architectural fixtures
and hardware

architectural fixtures and hardware

from faucets to flooring, storage to staircases,
the finest interior details for the home

MAGGIE STEVENSON *with photography by* CHRIS EVERARD

RYLAND
PETERS
& SMALL

LONDON NEW YORK

Senior designer **Sally Powell**

Senior editor **Sophie Bevan**

Location research **Kate Brunt and Georgia Stratton**

Picture researcher **Emily Westlake**

Production **Tamsin Curwood**

Art director **Gabriella Le Grazie**

Publishing director **Alison Starling**

First published in the USA in 2002
by Ryland Peters & Small, Inc
519 Broadway, 5th Floor
New York, NY 10012
www.rylandpeters.com

10 9 8 7 6 5 4 3 2 1

Library of Congress Cataloging-in-Publication Data

Stevenson, Maggie.
    Architectural fixtures and hardware : from faucets to flooring, storage to staircases, the finest interior details for the home / Maggie Stevenson with photography by Chris Everard.
        p. cm.
    Includes index.
    ISBN 1-84172-324-X
    1. Interior architecture. 2. Interior decoration. I. Everard, Chris. II. Title.

    NA2850 .S74 2002
    729--dc21
                              2002024948

CONTENTS

introduction

Architectural details define and underline the style of a home. They can be seen in the fabric of the building—the walls, ceilings, windows, and staircases—where they create a context for the decorating scheme. And they are there in the finishing touches—the door handles, light fixtures, faucets, and tiles—without which no scheme would gel. Most of these things are interesting or beautiful in their own right, many fulfill a specific function, but it is always the way they are used and their appropriateness to the scheme that is important.

Architects and designers know where to find the materials and fixtures they need to create or restore interesting interiors, and in this book, they reveal their sources. Eclectic in their shopping habits, they will buy as readily from chain and hardware stores as from specialized suppliers, so if the item you want is not listed in the directory at the back of this book, you could easily find it in a local outlet. Some of the names in the directory are trade suppliers who do not sell direct to the public, but will deal with the builder or contractor you employ. Usually items are only made available to the trade because specialized knowledge is needed for their installation. Obviously, complex lighting systems and structural features such as staircases require specialized specification and installation, but even something as apparently straightforward as a marble counter for a kitchen is best left to an experienced contractor since inaccurate measuring could be an expensive mistake.

Because individual outlets will be inaccessible to the majority of readers, most of the items are listed in the directory under the name of their manufacturer. Most manufacturers (but not all) deal only with retailers, but should be able to direct you to a mail-order supplier or a local store where you can buy their products. If the manufacturer is based overseas, call or check their website for details of agents or suppliers in the United States. Makers who do not have international distribution may be willing to ship their products overseas, but (with electrical and plumbing products in particular) make sure you will be able to install them safely and legally when they arrive.

Some products become recognized as design classics because they combine form and function successfully and strike a chord with contemporary taste. Favored by architects and designers, you'll see them crop up in different settings throughout this book. Often, these classics are not as contemporary as they look and were conceived by Modernist architects and designers in the mid-20th century. One advantage of their enduring popularity is that they are likely to remain in production for the foreseeable future, while designs with a less distinguished pedigree will be superseded or simply disappear.

Designers restoring period buildings often frequent architectural salvage yards in their search for authentic fixtures. Although they are a reliable source, the quality of merchandise is variable, and it pays to establish whether the item you are buying is complete and in working order, because spare parts and an experienced repairer may be hard to find later on. If absolute authenticity is not a priority, some of the larger salvage specialists sell reproduction pieces—specifically radiators, bathroom fixtures and brassware—copied from originals that have passed through their hands.

This book is intended to be as much a source of inspiration as information. The images offer hundreds of ideas for imaginative interiors, while the directory will help you realize them.

DOORS & WINDOWS

DOORS AND WINDOWS ARE INTEGRAL TO A HOUSE. PART OF ITS ORIGINAL

CONCEPTION, THEY ARE DESIGNED IN PROPORTION TO ITS SIZE AND FASHIONED

TO COMPLEMENT ITS CHARACTER. IN MOST CASES THERE IS LITTLE TO BE

GAINED FROM ALTERING THESE FEATURES, AND SOMETIMES MUCH TO BE LOST.

HOWEVER, IN HOMES THAT ARE BEING EXTENDED OR CONVERTED, OR ARE

UNDERGOING A RADICAL REDESIGN OF THE INTERNAL SPACE, NEW DOORS AND

WINDOWS CAN UNDOUBTEDLY IMPROVE THE LIVING SPACE.

doorways

The front door is the main feature in the façade of a house and is designed in proportion to the building—consider the narrow doors of tall rowhouses, the wide doors of Victorian homes and the broad flat canopies and flush doors of 20th-century Modernist houses. Factors determining the proportions of interior doors are slightly different, being as much to do with the importance and purpose of the rooms they connect as with the style of the building.

above left **Double doors make an imposing entrance, but these understated doors are at one with the quietly contemporary hall.**
above center **A huge single door, its thickness in proportion to its size, pivots slightly off-center, converting an existing archway into a doorway.**
above right **Due to its exaggerated height, this double doorway has the proportions of a standard contemporary single door.**

The door is the first feature of any house, apartment, or room with which you make direct contact. You focus on it as you approach, see it at close quarters, and then touch it as you enter. How it looks, feels, and works are key to the way it integrates with its surroundings and to the first impression you have of the space you are entering.

Size is the first thing you notice about a door, and this factor may be decided for practical or aesthetic reasons—ideally, both will be taken into consideration. In a beach house, for example, the doors may be small to conserve heat. By contrast, in a converted industrial building, they will be larger than usual to allow for the passage of goods, machinery, and the increased traffic of a workplace. In townhouses, the conventional format for doors—developed from the 18th-century classical rules of proportion—required the height of a door to be a little more than twice its width. Now there are no such limitations, and though the standard size is more likely to be two-and-a-half times taller than it is wide, doors can be made to order in any shape or size.

Conventionally, the doors of the most important and public rooms—usually those leading off the foyer—were the largest, heaviest, and most decorative, possibly including a wide architrave, molded paneling, and sometimes pilasters and pediments. The doors on upper floors, less often seen by guests, were much simpler. Such conventions may seem anachronistic in a modern home, but although times have changed the status factor still holds good, and living-room doors tend to be more impressive in size, style, or quality than in other rooms.

door styles & materials

At one time doors were made from oak and little else, but later softwoods such as fir, spruce, and pine became the norm and were frequently painted to imitate costlier lumbers. Now, the materials used to make doors are much more varied, with softwoods, hardwoods, plywoods, metal, and glass all competing for popularity.

opposite, above left **Separating a loft apartment from the central staircase, this Japanese-inspired sliding door has an ash frame glazed with a single pane of glass and suspended from a beam.**

opposite, above right **The vertical lights in this door are in Arts and Crafts style. The glazing bars of the outward-opening exterior door are similarly geometric.**

opposite, below left **A flush sliding door glides across a wide doorway. The recessed pull is the only interruption to the smooth expanse of door and wall.**

opposite, below center **Over-doors—decorative wood pediments—were a familiar feature in prosperous British houses of the late 19th century. This one is** taller than usual and forms part of a set of carved paneling in a house of the Aesthetic Movement.

opposite, below right **This red oak door was custom designed by Mark Pynn with square panels to reflect a square motif used elsewhere in the house. The doorknob, made from oil-rubbed bronze, conforms to this theme with a specially made square escutcheon.**

this page, below left **In hot climates or summer, the heat of direct sun through glazed doors is unwelcome. In this Singapore house a louvered panel, its vanes set in the horizontal position, holds the balance of light and heat, allowing most light to pass through when the sun is low in the sky.**

this page, below center **An unusual surface for an interior wall, these horizontal planks with the bark left on give a modern rustic look. Continued across the door with perfect alignment, the camouflage is so effective that when the door is closed, the door handle is the only obvious clue to its presence.**

this page, below right **These country-style doors belong to a house that was once a working farm building. The old doors, in too poor a condition to salvage, were copied exactly, but the lintel above the door has survived intact and still bears the original whitewash. The paint color chosen for the doors is Powder Blue by Farrow & Ball.**

left **Old, but probably not original to the 18th-century house in which it is found, this four-paneled door, painted soft gray-blue, is typically Victorian in style.**

below left **Tongue-and-groove paneling is not usually associated with contemporary interiors, but by painting the wall boards a dramatically dark color and the door pale cream, the scheme separates into modern blocks of contrasting color.**

below center **Painting the doors and walls on this landing the same sunny yellow gives a sense of space and continuity, with white architraves providing sparking highlights. Unusually, the doors have thumb latches instead of knobs—a detail that lends a rustic touch.**

below right **Derived from the abstract paintings of the American artist Ellsworth Kelly, the arrowhead shape of this tangerine composite-board sliding door suggests movement.**

right **What strikes you first about the doors in this loft apartment is their color. The closet doors are made from light blue composite and the sliding door separating the living room from the corridor beyond is bright yellow. However, the most interesting thing is that the living-room door is approved as a fireproof door—most unusual for sliding doors. When it is closed, a weight-and-pulley system pushes the solid-core wooden door against seals hidden within the door frame, rendering it smokeproof.**

The most popular modern wooden doors are those in softwood or solid or veneered hardwood. They may have clear or translucent glass panels to allow light to spill from room to room. Others are made from plywood in a hollow box construction or from a composite-board material, which provides a perfectly smooth base for a painted finish and can be cut into unconventional shapes. Metal frames have been a feature of external doors since the 1930s, and the pioneering British manufacturer Crittall is still in existence today producing metal door and window frames in similar patterns to the originals, for those renovating Moderne houses or adopting that style.

Large metal-framed exterior doors containing a single pane of glass often form part of contemporary houses and extensions, allowing daylight to pour in and enhancing the feeling of space by visually merging the interior and exterior. Internal glass doors usually have a wood or metal frame and solid glazing bars to indicate their

this page, above **The entrance to this room within a room is more movable wall than door and, when closed, there is no obvious point of access. The sandblasted glass panels are held in aluminum frames, two of which slide on small castors along tracks recessed into the floor.**

this page, below **These pivoting double-glazed "barn doors" by Metal UK span one end of a living room. The narrow galvanized-steel frames emphasize the double square shape and are appropriately discreet in a room with no baseboards or other applied decoration.**

opposite, above left **Sliding doors with dark mahogany frames and white glass panels have an oriental appearance reminiscent of Japanese shoji screens.**

opposite, above center and right **Sliding doors in the glass walls of this garden pavilion pull back wide to unite the indoor and outdoor spaces. When the sun is at its height, Venetian blinds drop down over doors and walls. Flush hardware gives a smooth finish: the sliding track fits level with the floor and the the lock is recessed into the aluminum frame.**

opposite, center left **The Kyoto sliding partition by Eclectics is made from sheer fabric panels to bring a feeling of openness. More a screen than a door, it defines rather than encloses space.**

opposite, below left **Crittall steel doors usually have a distinctly retro look. Here, however, there is a shift in perception as the bare galvanized metal harmonizes with the cool neutral tones of the materials in this modern kitchen.**

opposite, below right **Dark, handsome wenge—the designer wood of choice—forms the frame for translucent glass sliding doors. The materials link the two areas: the pearly sandblasted glass with the oyster-colored sofa; the dark wooden frame matches the hall furniture.**

presence. However, in some contemporary interiors, frameless panels of toughened and usually frosted glass are suspended from a sliding track on the ceiling as a sleek and minimalist alternative to the conventional hinged door.

Most doors are still hung on hinges and open in, but this arrangement can be reversed to give more usable space inside the room, provided there is enough space outside for the door to open safely. Doors that divide rooms are traditionally hinged in pairs, but again, if space is limited, bi-fold or sliding doors may be a more practical option. Sliding doors come into their own as room dividers: when they are closed, they offer privacy and bring the intimacy of individual rooms; opened up, they create expanded, sociable spaces for larger gatherings. However, they have the disadvantage of needing blank wall space, free of pictures and furniture, on which to open. One solution to this is to construct a false wall in front of the original one so the opening door slides between the two and is completely concealed when it is open.

top row, far left **Cabinet handles that pull to open must be shaped or textured so they do not slip through your fingers. The neat gray and nickel knobs on these cabinets are from the Forges line designed by Eero Aarnio for Valli and Valli, and have a velvety flat finish to provide a secure grip.**

top row, center left **A sliding door needs a flush handle, and when it is a bathroom door, the handle must be lockable, too. A recessed bathroom indicator bolt like this one by Merit Metal has one fold-flat handle to open the door and turn the lock.**

top row, center right **Projecting door handles can be annoying—and even hazardous—in a small bathroom where there is little space to undress or dry off. A flush ring handle—sometimes known as a squash-court ring—is a safe and stylish solution, and is available from Saturn Hardware.**

top row, near left **Cabinets and drawers in a contemporary kitchen require minimal but functional hardware that is in keeping with other furnishings in the room. This softly curved flat-finish nickel pull handle by Häfele fits the bill.**

handles & pulls

Hardware for doors and drawers is essentially functional, but alongside its main purpose it has an important stylistic role, too.

You'll know you've selected the right hardware for your home when you no longer notice it. Well-chosen hardware is visually in harmony with its surroundings, perfectly integrated with the door or furniture it opens and smoothly efficient in operation. Make the wrong choice and every time you enter a room or open a cupboard you will be aware of the jarring mismatch of style, the way the handle sticks when you turn it, or feels uncomfortable to hold. Instead of being automatic, the normal process of moving around your home and using the things in it will become an effort.

middle row, far left **Contracting materials add interest to a simple design. Components in the Sembla collection by Allgood, from which this propeller handle comes, are available in gray-finished, polished, or matte stainless steel, and can be combined in any permutation.**

middle row, center left **A wide contoured handle is comfortable to hold and looks good against a plain door. A modern classic designed by Johannes Potente in 1953, the 1020 design in aluminum or brass is from the FSB line by Allgood.**

middle row, center right **The slim, curved profile of this Ecostile satin chrome lever handle by Valli and Valli is in perfect visual balance with the glazed door.**

middle row, near left **Spherical doorknobs have a satisfying weight and substance, and suit modern and traditional doors. The brushed chrome 1023 ball mortice knob from Nu-line comes in a choice of finishes.**

bottom row, far left **Unusual handles can be made from fixtures designed for another purpose. In this kitchen, yacht cleats have been used on drawers and cupboards. Cleats are available from hardware stores.**

bottom row, center left **D-handles are universal. Available from all architectural suppliers, they come in a variety of sizes and finishes—from polished metal to colored nylon—and fit vertically or horizontally on doors and furniture alike.**

bottom row, center right **This leather handle matches the door panel and lends a masculine character to the piece. Beautifully engineered runners mean the leather is not put under too much stress.**

bottom row, near left **Quarter-round pulls are sturdy hardware for drawers storing heavy kitchen utensils. You'll find them in a variety of finishes at hardware and architectural suppliers. Bright chrome or a softer nickel finish give a modern look.**

windows

As natural portals for daylight and fresh air, windows are essential to our feeling of well-being. Viewed from the inside, they are a link between private space and the world outside, framing aspects of our surroundings in cameos that change with the time of day and the seasons. From the outside, they are probably the most distinctive feature of the buildings we inhabit, and they regulate the urban landscape with their repeating patterns.

Windows are part of the design of a building and essential to its integrity. If they are not a direct indicator of its age, status, and purpose, they are at least a clue. Most 18th- and 19th-century British houses were built with wooden sliding sash windows, but hinged casements returned to favor with the Arts and Crafts movement and were followed in the 1930s by steel casement windows. Plastic window frames appeared in the 1960s, but have never been able to shake off their budget image.

In older buildings, original windowpanes are as important and worthy of preservation as the frames that hold them, demonstrating their history by their gauge, color, and subtle grain. Old glass may not have the perfect, blemishfree clarity of modern glass, but the slight flaws within it cast rippling reflections on interior walls that bestow character and an atmosphere of calm.

Before technology allowed glass to be made in panes large enough to glaze picture windows, bay windows were built to allow more light to enter. By the 1930s, this concept had been refined in the shape of Suntrap windows, whose curved panes and streamlined, linear shape dominated popular domestic architecture. Now, glass technology allows windows to be made in any reasonable size. In modern houses,

above left **Casement windows are a typical feature of old working buildings, and though this studio is now a living space and office, the windows survive as evidence of its previous incarnations as a coach house and, it is said, a falconry. The frames are wooden, though metal ones are not unusual in such a situation, and the glass is reeded, which has a prismatic effect.**

above center **In houses which retain their original windows, their style is a useful guide to the age of the building. Sash windows became widespread in Britain and then the United States by the 1720s and remained fashionable** for around 200 years, but their shape and the arrangement of the panes varied throughout that time. The thin glazing bars and gothic detailing in these windows are typical of the early 19th century. Also typical are the internal shutters, which can be stored in the recessed shutter boxes at the sides by day.

above right **Oculi, or small round or oval windows, were a popular feature of 17th-century houses, and reappeared in 1930s Modernist houses as porthole windows. This one pivots to open, but others contain an opening square casement within the arrangement of glazing bars.**

where glass forms the skin of the building, it is hard to know where walls end and windows begin. For the person inside, there is no confusion: the walls are windows.

With double-glazing and central heating to take care of the practicalities of keeping warm, it is easy to understand the attractions of a house where most of the walls are glazed. The view, the light, and the feeling of space are undeniably seductive, but on the downside are the feeling of exposure and the contradiction of being within a landscape but separated from it. In houses within a rural or seaside landscape, the problem of being on display is less pressing than in town, as large windows and glass walls are usually positioned to gaze onto an open aspect where development is unlikely or impossible. In town, where privacy is a rarer commodity, careful orientation and screening with trees, hedges, or high walls or fences is the answer. The feeling of separation that comes from viewing an outdoor landscape from behind glass is easy to dispel by creating a middle ground between inside and outside in the shape of a balcony, deck, or terrace. Doors from the living area opening directly onto this space allow the scents and sounds of the garden, sea or countryside to be enjoyed with the view.

opposite, above left **Metal-framed windows with pivoting casements were once common in schools, hospitals, the service areas of some houses, and industrial buildings, like this converted factory. The frames are now glazed with frosted panes that give a clean groomed look, block the view without resort to blinds, and diffuse light into the bright white interior.**

opposite, above center **One advantage of high-rise living is that windows can be left uncurtained to give spectacular views without compromising privacy. At night, when the scene changes to an illuminated cityscape, this contemporary apartment is placed securely in its urban context. The squared grid of mullions and transoms echoes the angular style of the furniture and is therefore an important element of the room's design, but some may find bare windows uncomfortable and prefer to soften the effect with gauzy, translucent blinds or shades.**

opposite, center **Although the strong horizontal bias of this wall of windows recalls the Modernist architecture of the 1930s, it actually forms part of a house designed in the last decade by Moore Ruble Yudell. With the Pacific Ocean on one side and a highway on the other, the decision to build the beachside aspect almost entirely of glass was easy to reach. The windows slide back to give access to a wide wooden deck, creating a huge open living area, while the horizontal panes and the deck rail outside add a strong nautical flavour.**

opposite, above right **A single, dramatic architectural feature can transform any building, however modest, into a local landmark. This tiny house in a leafy Parisian courtyard was converted from a 19th-century storeroom by architect Damien Roland. Originally windowless, it has been made light by replacing sections of roof and wall with glass. Most striking of all these insertions is a huge circular window above the entrance which, at night, glows like a harvest moon through the trees.**

opposite, below **The living area of this house, designed by Sidnam Petrone Gartner and set in the wooded landscape of upstate New York, is enclosed by glass, making the already lofty space seem even greater. The boundary may be transparent, but its steel structure is apparent, dividing the glass into panels of different sizes, each framing a detail of the surroundings.**

above right **A series of tall, slender panels forms a shimmering crescent of glass that is part wall, part window. A wall in as much as it forms a permanent and immovable division between house and garden; a window by virtue of the view it gives of the lawn and the countryside beyond. The curve of glass allows daylight to flood the indoor living space of this family home designed by Ken Shuttleworth.**

center right **The panoramic view at the junction of two glazed walls makes a strong connection between house and forest, but switch your focus to the regular framework of the structure and the distinction between civilized space and wilderness becomes apparent. In summer, the glass is shaded by the trees, but in winter, sun filters through the bare branches to brighten the room through the daylight hours.**

below right **Few homes enjoy such a broad, uninterrupted sea view, so this one exploits its position with a wall of glass. The horizontal panes continue across the wall and door, emphasizing the strong parallel lines of the shore, wall, and horizon.**

above far left **Light entering this dining room is filtered first through foliage and then through the frosted windowpanes to give the space a bright but cool atmosphere. The window itself is left uncurtained, its regular geometry providing a framework for the shadow-show of plants brushing its outside surface.**

above center **A wall of floor-to-ceiling windows can restrict the arrangement of furniture, but here the windows are raised from the floor, permitting low furniture to be placed below sill level. The long, narrow window accentuates the length of the room, an effect exaggerated by the dark fascia above.**

above **Daylight and privacy do not always go hand in hand, but in this bedroom a solution has been found by obscuring the central panels of glass in the window wall with frosted glass and constructing part of the flanking wall with glass bricks. Both materials screen the view effectively but otherwise have quite different effects: the frosted glass diffuses the light so it appears bright even on cloudy days; the bricks create rippling watery reflections when the light glints through them.**

left **The wall of glass separating the interior of this house from the terrace is virtually frameless. Rising from ground to ceiling with no visible means of attachment to either, the panels are joined side by side with the narrowest of vertical supports and are fixed and permanent. Outside, a slatted canopy overhangs the roof to shade the glass, and though it protects the interior from glare efficiently, the bars of shadow it casts on the terrace suggest pure heat.**

opposite, above left **Glass-to-glass assembly, the panes joined with narrow seams of mastic, means this fixed skylight offers a clear view of the sky.**

opposite, above center **In an internal room, the shock of light from a large skylight is dramatic. The effect is heightened in this hall by leaving the room virtually bare of furniture, with a large oil painting as the only decoration.**

opposite, above right **A huge skylight means this studio apartment is always well lit. The sleeping platform suspended beneath it acts as a baffle, protecting the space from direct sun. Operated by remote control, the skylight by Sunfold Systems opens for ventilation and to give access to the roof.**

opposite, below **VX Design and Architecture installed this large skylight to define the dining area in a free-flowing living space. A box containing storage and the exhaust vent lowers the ceiling over a kitchen island and provides hanging space for a grass painting by Andy Harper.**

above right **This steel-framed glass roof is motorized to slide back and forth, transforming the dining room it covers into an indoor–outdoor space. Even closed, its glazed sloping sides provide good light all day as the sun moves across the sky.**

above far right **This extension is built in a familiar lean-to style, but that is where resemblance to any traditional construction ends. The exterior wall is a seamless pane, and the sloping glass roof supported by beams of laminated glass. At ground level, sections of the floor have been replaced with glazed strips to act as skylights for the basement.**

below right **A dining extension, built to mirror the adjoining kitchen, has matching steel-framed Crittall doors and a glass roof, designed and made by a conservatory company.**

skylights

By opening a room to the heavens, skylights admit maximum daylight and give the appearance of expanding the interior space.

The installation of a window in the roof is a sure way to fill the room below with natural light. Causing less visual disruption to the architecture than an additional window in the building's façade, and much less likely to be overshadowed by trees or overlooked by neighbors, it admits light throughout the day. Skylights take many forms, from a simple polycarbonate dome admitting a shaft of light into a dark landing to a large panel replacing a section of the roof. Some skylights are stationary, but as extra sunlight inevitably results in increased heat, ventilation is essential for a comfortable environment. The Velux windows often used in attic remodeling open easily on a pivot, but other types are hinged or slide open. The inaccessibility of high windows means that a special opening system will be needed—this can be manually or electrically operated or automatically controlled by thermostat. Horizontal or sloping skylights must contain laminated or toughened safety glass to protect against damage from high winds or falling masonry, and where overheating is a particular problem, tinted or solar-reflective glass will reduce the sun's glare.

blinds & shutters

Blinds or shutters are good choices for window coverings, controlling light and giving privacy without obscuring the architectural features.

First conceived to protect furnishings from fading in sunlight and as a security measure, shutters can be made to measure for modern windows with set or pivoting louvers or solid panels.

Blinds offer enormous scope across their range. Roll-up shades are the cheapest and easiest option, and come in a variety of materials to give the perfect balance of light and privacy. Venetian blinds are also flexible, with slats that can be adjusted to control the influx of light. Slats come in various widths, materials, and finishes to suit virtually any size or style of window.

above **Metallic Venetian blinds are a good choice of window treatment for a kitchen, where steel and aluminum surfaces predominate. Narrow slats suit the proportions of a small window.**

near right **In a kitchen with one long wall of window, a purpose-made screen composed of etched-glass panels obscures the view and reduces glare. Each panel is separately mounted on steel brackets and pivots to alter the balance of light, but even when closed, the effect is cool and translucent.**

far right **Venetian blinds drop down over the glass walls and sliding doors of a garden pavilion to cool the interior on sunny days and give the walls solidity when the seclusion of an enclosed space is required. Separate blinds allow the doorway to be left open while the windows remain covered.**

below near right **In addition to dividing external and internal spaces, blinds can form a boundary within a room to give a degree of visual separation. Here a wooden Venetian blind is hung from a beam to screen the entrance from the living room without losing any sense of space.**

below far right **A city-center apartment won't always have a pleasing outlook and, tilted just enough to allow light to enter, the half-opened slats of a Venetian blind are a stylish visual distraction from the view.**

opposite **Pivoting curves of birch-veneered glass are an architect's solution to the problem of screening a huge window overlooking city rooftops while maintaining the level of light. At night the effect is not lost, as fine fluorescent tubes concealed within the panels take the place of daylight.**

FLOORING

AFTER THE WALLS AND CEILING, THE FLOOR IS THE LARGEST SURFACE IN A ROOM. WHETHER COVERED OR LEFT BARE, ITS STYLE, COLOR, AND TEXTURE WILL EXERT A STRONG INFLUENCE ON THE WIDER DECORATIVE SCHEME. OF EQUAL IMPORTANCE IS THE WAY THE FLOOR FEELS. IT IS THE ONE SURFACE WITH WHICH WE MAKE DIRECT CONTACT MOST OF THE TIME. WE WALK ON IT, SIT ON IT, STEP OUT OF BED ONTO IT—SO, SOFT OR SMOOTH, IT MUST BE COMFORTABLE AND PLEASANT TO TOUCH.

hard flooring

Claimed as the surface of choice for contemporary interiors, hard floors—from mellow flagstones to shiny metal, smooth terrazzo to chunky cobblestones—have a long history.

Natural stone and ancient manmade materials like brick, mosaic, terracotta, and ceramic have been used in ordinary homes for thousands of years and are still relevant today. Marble, slate, and granite endowed the grand houses of the past with a sense of stability and sophistication, and now bring those qualities to modern homes. Even concrete and metal, once deemed too utilitarian for domestic life, have been embraced by designers for their practicality and urban aesthetic. Add to these the glamorous terrazzo floors, frequently used in stores and hotels, but equally appropriate at home, and the newly developed textural resin-based materials that mimic graveled outdoor surfaces, and the list of hard floor options is longer than ever before.

   All hard floors are rigid and comparatively heavy, so they must be laid on a level, stable subfloor strong enough to bear the weight. A solid concrete base is ideal, but wooden floors, properly reinforced and leveled, can provide a firm foundation. If there is any risk of movement in the subfloor that could cause tiles or stones to crack,

above far left **More often seen in commercial interiors, terrazzo makes a very hardwearing floor, performing well in living rooms and other busy areas of the home. This example, a warm honey color, is semi-polished and fully sealed to give a low-maintenance satin finish. With underfloor heating, it is comfortable to walk on in winter and refreshingly cool in summer.**
above center left **Smooth gray-green stone, like this Brazilian Camborne slate, has a matte surface that is durable, easy to maintain, and perfect for through routes such as halls and stairs. Had the steps been constructed entirely from gray slate, the effect would have been dark and heavy, but alternating slate treads with white-painted risers gives definition to the steps and a lighter, sharper look.**
above center **Unpolished concrete is a sympathetic material for a modern country interior and a hardwearing nonslip choice for a hallway and staircase. Its gray-beige color complements neutral schemes and provides a quiet background against which stronger colors can stand out.**
above center right **Slate is a supremely versatile surfacing**

material and can be applied to vertical and horizontal surfaces in both wet and dry areas. In this contemporary bathroom, gleaming green slate tiles cover the floor, and larger panels line the shower enclosure to give continuity. Stone surfaces can be slippery when wet, so use mats inside and outside the shower.
above far right **More often seen as an outdoor surface, these beach pebbles set into cement make an unusual cobbled floor for a bathroom. As long as the stones chosen are smooth, rounded, and do not stand up too high, they will be pleasantly stimulating to walk on with bare feet.**
near right, above and below **Chips of marble set in resin produce a continuous floor with a granular but level surface that is extremely durable. Laid in situ, the pale, slightly sparkling surface reflects light, making the room seem brighter and more spacious.**
far right **Metal flooring consolidates the retro-commercial design of this stylish home-work space furnished largely with vintage office furniture. In such a setting, the material's two main disadvantages—that it is slippery when wet and noisy underfoot—are not major concerns.**

above far left **Tough and elemental, a concrete floor is appropriate for an industrial-style kitchen, adding to its workmanlike style. The smooth, compacted "polished" finish is achieved by power-troweling the wet concrete during installation. This is best done during the construction (ideally, before the walls are built) or during a major refurbishment of the building. When the floor is completely dry, a seal may be applied to protect against dirt and grease.**

above center **Pale Batigue Blue limestone tiles from Granite & Marble International present a cool background for modern metal furniture. The tiles extend through to the kitchen where, for continuity, a countertop has been made from the same stone.**

above near left **A favorite flooring for stores, office foyers, cafés, and other public areas, stylish, durable terrazzo is a good choice for the home, too. Terrazzo tiles are easy to lay and give a uniform color and pattern.**

below far left **The mellow tones of brick paviors guarantee their popularity in traditional homes, but in a brighter shade of red, laid in an unconventional arrangement, and edged with a contrasting material such as white marble, they take on a much more contemporary look.**

below center **Smooth terrazzo, laid in situ, is an elegant flooring for an open-plan space. It is practical in the kitchen and looks sleek in the living area, where rugs will soften its sometimes austere appearance. Installation is a professional job: the wet cement and aggregate mix is spread onto a stable subfloor, then ground and polished to a satiny finish. The resulting floor requires little maintenance beyond sweeping and occasional mopping.**

below near left **Not just for utilitarian areas, pale concrete provides a sophisticated base for a modern neutral scheme. The surface must be sealed to protect it from dust, but a flat finish gives it a softer appearance.**

expansion joints can be incorporated. Don't economize on installation; the standard of preparation and finish has a bearing on the life expectancy of a hard floor as well as its appearance. Where the bedding material offers poor support or the joints are uneven, tiles and stones will eventually crack, chip, or crumble.

The main problem associated with hard flooring is that it feels chilly underfoot, but this can be solved by underfloor heating. Installing this type of heating need not cause major disruption. Often an existing central-heating system can be adapted or extended to provide it or, if the room in question is a bathroom or other small room, an electric under-tile system can be put in independent from the main central heating. Once the floor is warm, the whole surface radiates a low level of heat, providing the room with a comfortable, even temperature.

If you're considering hard flooring, you will already have an idea of the effect you want to achieve, but factors other than style must be taken into account when you decide what flooring material to

top left **Old terracotta tiles are more often inherited than acquired, and a chequerboard floor has a time-worn charm worth preserving. Resist any temptation to protect old tiles with a waterproof seal, because moisture rising through the porous clay will cause the surface finish to deteriorate.**

top center **A variation of terrazzo, this highly decorative flooring is made from Japanese river pebbles set into concrete, then ground smooth. Its polished, randomly patterned surface contrasts with the plain pale wood alongside it. Similar pebble flooring is made to order by Steve Charles.**

above left **A classic flooring pattern of light-colored octagonal tiles linked by small dark keystones can be interpreted in stone or ceramic, and in varying proportions, to produce different effects.**

above center **Colorful Victorian tessellated floors demonstrate the decorative possibilities of combining tiles of different shapes, but this floor gives the idea a modern slant by restricting the design to two colors and shapes, and concentrating on the geometry of a "tumbling blocks" patchwork. Similar terracotta tiles are available from Paris Ceramics.**

main picture and right **Frostproof terracotta tiles can be used inside or out, and when continued through French doors onto a terrace, they appear to extend the living space. Small patterned inset tiles add points of color to the floor and allow a more interesting stepped layout. Large terracotta tiles are widely available and 2-inch- (50-mm-) square glazed inset tiles from Turkey and Mexico are available from a selection at Fired Earth. As glazed tiles are less**

hardwearing than clay, they should be slightly countersunk to reduce the wear they get.

opposite, above right **These new cement tiles have a darkly subtle color and dead-flat finish that gives an impression of great age. The central motif, quartered at the corners, is a traditional device in tile design that results in a regular pattern when the tiles are laid. Made in Morocco, they are designed by Agnès Emery for Emery & Cie.**

opposite, below right **Grid designs of greater detail and definition can be produced with smaller tiles. These tiles, smaller than standard size but larger than mosaic, have a slightly metallic glaze which, together with the black border, gives a crisp look. Similar 1⅞-inch- (47-mm-) square tiles are available from the Pro Architectura line by Villeroy & Boch.**

buy. Cost is always important, and with stone and tiles, the price per square yard is only part of the story. To get an accurate forecast, your calculations should include the cost of preparing the subfloor, laying the floor, and, if necessary, sealing it.

Practicality is another deciding factor. Be aware of the characteristics of different flooring materials, and be realistic about how your intended floor will perform in the setting you have in mind. Granite and marble are hardwearing, but marble can be marked by acids, and refinishing it is a professional job. Both are considered luxury materials and priced accordingly, so they are generally used in areas where their sophisticated good looks can be fully appreciated. Slate is another hardwearing stone, and is waterproof and stain resistant. More affordable than granite or marble and appropriate for both traditional and contemporary settings, it can be used to great effect in spaces such as kitchens, halls and staircases. All hard stones may be polished, but the higher the gloss, the more slippery the surface, especially when wet.

Softer stones like limestone and sandstone come in elegant neutral colors that are easy to live with. They are, however, porous and will stain if not sealed. Tiles vary in character and performance according to their type and quality. Bricks, terracotta, and quarry tiles are all hardwearing, relatively inexpensive, easy to maintain, and seem to improve in appearance with age and use. Traditionally used for kitchen flooring, they work well in other downstairs areas where a rustic look is desired. Glazed tiles can look spectacularly colorful, but not all are tough enough to provide a durable floor surface, so check before you buy. Less robust tiles

opposite **An area of glass floor situated directly beneath a large roof light allows daylight to reach the basement of this potentially dark two-level building remodelled by architect Damien Roland. Although clear glass admits maximum light, it can be disconcerting to walk on so, to give a sense of solidity without losing light, the clear glass panels inserted into a central section of the floor were surrounded with more substantial -looking semi-opaque glass bricks. Viewed from below, the clear glass floor panels appear as a skylight, banishing the gloom so often associated with subterranean rooms. From above, the eye can rest on the surface, watching reflections, or gaze through it to glimpse the activity in the basement.**

above left **In a small mews house designed by architects McDowell & Benedetti, a glass walkway linking the upper rooms illuminates the enclosed staircase**

below with daylight and gives a lofty, spacious feel to the ground floor. To counter the slipperiness of the glass—and any feeling of stepping into the void—a series of friction bars has been sandblasted into its surface.

center left **Designed as a showcase for shells and corals gathered in the West Indies, this floor is composed of white-painted boxes held within a steel frame, each covered with laminated glass. The boxes are lit by concealed fittings and the glass can be lifted, using glaziers' suction pads, to allow the contents to be rearranged.**

below left **There are situations where semi-opaque glass is more appropriate than clear. It gives privacy, defines boundaries and diffuses light, reducing glare. Irregular panels of ice-green frosted glass form the walls and floor of this passageway so it benefits from light entering from below and from adjoining rooms without affording a clear view in.**

can be used in bathrooms where they will not suffer excessive wear, but wall tiles should never be used on the floor.

Terrazzo and polished concrete floors are durable enough to perform well in most areas of the home, but installing them is specialized work and best done when a building is being constructed or during major refurbishment. Terrazzo tiles, which are thinner and lighter than in-situ terrazzo, can be laid with much less disruption and give a similar effect.

Metal floors have become more accessible with the advent of floor tiles, but if you are choosing sheet metal, it must be firmly anchored to a level subfloor. Metal is very slippery when wet and should only be used in dry areas, or for decorative effect in combination with another flooring material.

Glass floors look stunning, creating a feeling of space and allowing light to pass through different levels of a building. They are made from layers of annealed float glass (as opposed to sheet or plate glass) laminated together to provide the required strength. The surface is then sandblasted to render it slip resistant. Glass floors should always be professionally specified and installed.

above left **A hard, closely grained lumber, Canadian maple is often used for flooring in areas of heavy wear, so is perfect for busy areas of a home. Available from specialized suppliers, it can vary in color from pale cream to brown—sometimes with a pinkish tone like the floor in this sunny room—depending on the part of the tree from which the wood was cut. The highest grade of maple is very light in color with few, if any, small knots.**

above center **The honey-colored beech flooring installed in the living area of this open-plan loft apartment contrasts in color and texture with the Treadmaster cork-and-rubber material in the kitchen beyond. Made by Junckers, the beech flooring overlays existing old pine floorboards. An expanded foam sheet between the two gives resilience and adds a degree of sound insulation.**

left **Plywood often displays a more exuberant grain than ordinary planks and can be cut into much wider boards, which, in turn, show off its wonderful**

wooden flooring

Wooden flooring has never gone out of style. Its warm color and flowing grain present a surface that is easy on the eye, warm underfoot, and a versatile background for a variety of decorating styles. It occupies the middle ground between hard and soft flooring. More forgiving, resilient, and quieter than stone or ceramic, and cooler and airier than carpet—wood offers the best of both worlds.

The wonderful thing about wood is its variety. It comes in natural tones ranging from white blond through every shade of brown to almost black, with a similarly wide diversity of grain patterns, depending on the species of tree. Versatile in use, it can be laid in planks, strips, or blocks in any number of geometric patterns, or used as the raw material for other wood products such as plywood and blockboard. It can reveal its own grain or be stained or painted to give color.

Like most natural materials, wood improves with age, acquiring a deeper, more mellow tone, and old wood floors, scrubbed or waxed, complement traditional, rustic, and contemporary interiors alike. In an old house, the easiest and cheapest way to acquire an old wood floor is simply to take up the carpets and expose the existing boards. Restoring old floorboards is not complicated, but it is hard work; and if you don't wish to tackle it yourself, you can hire an experienced company to do the job. Provided the boards are free of rot or insect attack, are reasonably level, and do not have wide gaps between them, the restoration process is simply a matter of securing loose boards, sanding the surface, and sealing it with one of the many commercial solvent- or water-based products available. If it is necessary to replace damaged boards, reclaimed ones from an architectural salvage center may be a closer match in terms of color, width, and thickness than new. Old parquet floors can be restored in much the same way, but the blocks should be sanded in the direction of the grain to give a smooth finish.

pattern. A heavily figured plywood like this Wisa spruce is most effective in a large room where its lively design, enriched and emphasized by a polyurethane lacquer finish, will not overwhelm the space.
above **Reclaimed woodblock flooring gives a room instant character. Here it has been laid in a brick arrangement instead of the usual herringbone or basketweave pattern. Architectural salvage specialists usually stock blocks in a variety of woods, including pine, oak, beech, and mahogany, but often they need to be cleaned of old adhesive before being relaid.**
right **Wide boards give an expansive look, enhanced in this minimalist space by continuing the wood up to form a plinth for the cabinets that extend the length of the room. The 8-inch-(200-mm-) wide beech laminate boards were specially made, but can be ordered from Mafi. The raised platform at the end of the room is made from light gray limestone which complements the warm color of the wood.**

left **The segmented floor in this curved hallway is made from composite-board panels painted chocolate brown. The edges of each panel have been chamfered to accentuate the radiating joints.**

opposite, above left **Blockboard is more often laid as a smooth base for another flooring, but these tiles—part of a floor-leveling system made by Kingspan Access Floors—have been lacquered and left uncovered. The tiles are supported on "feet" that can be adjusted to compensate for irregularities in the floor surface. Galvanized metal hardware is visible at the corners of each tile and contrast nicely with the brown board.**

opposite, above center **Old floors, whether original or salvaged, will lose some of their antique character if over-restored. Avoid aggressive sanding and be prepared to live with a slightly uneven surface and some gaps between boards. Maintain a natural look by scrubbing and waxing the boards or sealing with a clear flat varnish.**

opposite, above right **Sterling board, a coarse-grained form of blockboard, may not be as durable as some solid or laminated wood floors, but its warm golden color and cork-like appearance are attractive, and it costs a fraction of the price of solid wood. Because of its weight, tiles are easier to handle than larger panels.**

opposite, main **Light oak boards in a room with a coastal view echo the color of the sand. Although the tone is uniform, the boards are of differing widths to give a more interesting effect. Strong, durable, pest- and rot-resistant, and with a pleasing grain, oak is a classic flooring wood and looks wonderful in a contemporary setting.**

left and below left **A double border of darker wood inset in a parquet floor outlines the shape of this hall and lends distinction to the pine woodblocks.**

bottom left **Reclaimed narrow woodblocks have been laid in rows and thoroughly sanded for a perfectly smooth, level, and unusually striped floor.**

below right **End-grain woodblocks are supremely durable (they were used for the treads of 19th-century railroad bridges and,** more recently, in the foyer at the **Barbican Theatre in London). These are made from smoked oak—a rich dark wood.**

bottom right **Parquet is usually glued in place, but if it must be nailed down, the nails should be perfectly aligned.**

right **Practical, hardwearing and attractive, oak parquet extends throughout this basement kitchen and living area. The pale-toned wood was chosen to blend with the softly muted color scheme.**

If the existing floorboards in your home are in very poor condition or you want something other than pine boards, consider reclaimed flooring. This tends to be salvaged from industrial premises, hospitals, and schools that contained large quantities of wood, so it is not difficult to buy enough for a room in a house. The wood may be clean and ready to use, but often it is sold "as found," so you should allow for wastage where boards or blocks are damaged or stained.

In a modern setting, the pristine finish and regularity of color and grain that new wood provides may be more appropriate than a time-worn look. Popular and widely available lumber includes pale hardwoods like maple, ash, and beech, which have a light, clean look, and cherry, walnut, and oak, which come in deeper wood tones. New wood flooring is sold in the form of solid boards, "engineered" plankwood, or as veneered boards.

Solid wood is the most expensive, but also the most durable. It comes in widths ranging from narrow strips to boards of 8 inches (200 mm) or more. When solid wood shows signs of wear and tear, it can be sanded and refinished.

Plankwood is composed of three layers. The top one, which varies in thickness depending on the maker, forms the surface of the finished floor; the central core consists of wood strips or blocks laid at right angles to this; and the lower layer runs in the same direction as the top. This type of floor is less expensive than solid wood, but it is extremely stable and can be made from woods that are prone to warping.

The cheapest of all real-wood options is a veneered floor. These consist of a thin layer of wood glued to a manufactured board and are supplied ready finished with a plasticized protective coating. If they become worn or damaged, they cannot be refinished.

Woodblock floors are very decorative. Traditional parquet comes in a number of configurations, from the familiar brick shapes arranged in herringbone or basketweave fashion to panels composed of geometric shapes like a wooden patchwork square. Wood mosaic blocks look like parquet in miniature, consisting of narrow strips of wood bonded onto a backing to form a wood tile. Much less expensive than real parquet, they are very easy to lay. End-grain woodblocks have an unusual and distinctive appearance and are highly durable.

Wood can be finished in a number of ways. Clear seals in flat or satin finish enhance the color of the wood slightly, but otherwise give a natural look. Wood stains come in a range of lumber shades, as well as some brighter colors, and permanently alter the color of the wood. Paint gives floors a solid-colored finish and covers marks and stains. Purpose-made floor paints are more durable than ordinary gloss or eggshell, but will eventually wear in doorways and other high-traffic areas. Repainting provides a quick and easy solution.

opposite **The parquet floor that extends across the living area of this apartment is a legacy of the old school from which it was converted. Too worn and damaged for repolishing, it was painted with three coats of Farrow & Ball floor paint in off-black Railings to give a very high-gloss finish.**
above left **It takes courage to choose bright red as an all-over floor color but in this living room it enlivens a predominantly neutral scheme. Red floor paints, ranging from terracotta through to scarlet, are available from specialized manufacturers.**
above center **Although the first impression is of color, painted wood floors have texture, too, as the shiny finish highlights the contours of the grain.**
above right **Several coats of varnish have deepened the color sheen of this dark wood floor and raised its surface to produce an effect similar to Chinese lacquer. Such a dramatic floor works best in a disciplined, architectural interior.**

right and below right **Rubber is one of the most durable floor coverings for busy areas, and regular polishing will maintain its good looks. Tiles come in various textures to give a slip-resistant surface. In addition to the familiar stud pattern, there is a choice of grid, basketweave, ribbed, and all-over designs.** far right **The brilliant blue studded tiles specified for this** colorful kitchen are Omega in Bleu Paon by Dalsouple. opposite **Modern materials cover every surface in this kitchen with a glossy poured epoxy floor. Plain white may not seem a practical choice for a busy kitchen, but poured flooring is self-leveling and perfectly smooth, so is easy to mop, and the pale reflective surface lends a light, airy atmosphere.**

sheet & soft tiling

Rubber, vinyl, and linoleum—long regarded as functional floorings—are now emerging from the kitchen to occupy new areas of the home. Chosen primarily for their durability and ease of care, these workhorse materials have an industrial aesthetic that makes them a popular choice for modern domestic interiors.

Smooth, resilient, and quiet, sheet flooring and soft tiling are the ultimate coverings for busy areas. They are warm and comfortable to stand on, a good choice for kitchens, where you spend a lot of time on your feet, and have an ease of care fitting to family life.

Price reflects durability. Treated with respect, the more expensive materials like linoleum, rubber, and high-quality vinyl will last for a decade or more. Cheaper vinyl and vinyl-faced cork tiles have a shorter life, but allow you to treat the floor as another element in a decorative scheme that can be changed without too great an outlay. Rubber is usually sold in tile form with a smooth or textured surface, in plain colors or patterns. Vinyl flooring comes in sheet or tile form, and is more often patterned than plain. The patterns

frequently simulate traditional materials such as wood, brick, and tile, but abstract modern designs are starting to appear. Linoleum, a natural material made from linseed oil and wood flour, comes in continuous sheets or as tiles, in a huge choice of solid or marbled colors. Where pattern is required, marquetrylike motifs and borders may be inset into the plain ground. Leather, a relative newcomer to the league of smooth flooring, is the wild card here. Far from utilitarian, it is expensive and luxurious, and although it wears well, it will stain and scratch if it is not treated with care.

above left **Once the utilitarian floor covering of kitchens and hospital corridors, linoleum has undergone a change of image. Available in a palette of marbled and solid colors, it can be inlaid with borders and motifs in standard or bespoke designs.**

above **Subtle variations in color are part of the charm of leather floor tiles. Their warm tones naturally complement modern and traditional furnishings.**

near left **Leather is one of the most sophisticated of floor coverings, and because it is warm and slightly giving to the touch, it is sensually appropriate for a contemporary bedroom. These tiles are from Bill Amberg.**

far left **Inlaid designs elevate linoleum from utility to designer status. A selection of ready-cut inset motifs and borders is available in Marmoleum by Forbo, or individual designs can be cut by a specialized installer.**

opposite, above left **Smooth, shiny and bright, rubber flooring makes a colorful impact in a bathroom. It is completely waterproof, but tends to be slippery when wet, so always use a bathmat.**

opposite, above right **An all-white bathroom may be the classic choice, but these rubber tiles by Dalsouple mean good taste need not be taken too seriously.**

opposite, below left **Slip-resistant textured vinyl is laid like a carpet down this flight of steps bringing a splash of color to a modern interior. Unlike cushioned vinyl, which is soft underfoot, textured sheet vinyl is highly durable and available in a wide choice of solid colors.**

opposite, below right **Rubber has a well-earned reputation as functional flooring. It now comes in such a choice of colors, as well as marbled and flecked designs, that, increasingly, it is valued for its decorative qualities.**

natural fibers & carpets

In rooms where comfort is the priority, soft flooring has never gone out of style. Warm and quiet underfoot, it envelops a room with a sense of luxury.

Soft flooring has a place in every home: in the bedroom it offers a sensual surface for bare feet; it cushions stairs and hallways against noise; and it provides a link for fabrics in the living room. Wall-to-wall carpet was once the universal choice, but now the field encompasses natural-fiber floor coverings, rugs, and runners. Of these, carpet offers the greatest choice of color, pattern, and texture, and comes in a variety of qualities to suit different levels of wear. Plain broadloom is an enduring classic, but neutral-toned cut-and-loop pile carpets and striped flat-weaves also have a strong following. If the wall-to-wall carpet has suffered from the vogue for hard floors, rugs have benefited. They provide a soft surface just where it is needed—by the bed, in front of the fireplace—and can add color to a neutral scheme.

Natural-fiber flooring such as coir, sisal, and jute is usually laid wall to wall. It comes in a range of natural colors and textured weaves that complement both contemporary and country-style furniture.

above far left **New to the ever-lengthening list of plant fibers used to make natural flooring, abaca is a product of the banana family. Softer and smoother-textured than most, with a beautiful silvery color, it is very durable and produces a satisfyingly chunky weave. Abaca rugs are available from Roger Oates Design.**

above center left **A graphic relief border carved into a thick pile rug by Christine Vanderhurd adds decoration without introducing another color to the scheme.**

above center top **The natural color of this herringbone coir flooring has an affinity with the rich vegetable-dyed colors of the kelim that lies over it.**

above center below **Made from rectangles of wool felt joined with blanket-stitched seams, this Tapis rug designed by Roger Oates in low-key colors makes an** unusual centerpiece for a contemporary room.

above center right **Natural flooring comes in a range of neutral tones and weaves. Here, rich brown bouclé sisal runs through from the lobby to the bedroom with a rough-hewn granite curbstone step marking the different level with a change of texture.**

above far right **The loop-and-pile grid pattern of this cream Target carpet by Stark Carpets has a crisp regularity that makes a suitably disciplined background for contemporary furniture.**

left **Custommade carpets—dyed, woven, inlaid or carved to order—are available for those with specific requirements. Borders are often incorporated into wall-to-wall carpets to emphasize the shape of a room, but this carpet, designed by Helen Yardley, has a sinuous "pathway" pattern of contrasting** color inset to lead the way through a gently curving entrance hall.

right **Texture affects the way color is perceived, and in this monochromatic carpet by Christine Vanderhurd, the disks of longer pile appear a shade darker than their close-cropped surroundings. Stud designs are common in utilitarian rubber flooring, so the same device interpreted in a much more luxurious material adds a note of elegant humor to a contemporary interior.**

below right **Modern rugs, like this example by Christopher Farr, are valued as works of art in their own right and can be the key to the color and style of a room. Placed at the center of a seating arrangement, they become a natural focus and receive as much attention as they would hung on the wall.**

WALLS & CEILINGS

WALLS AND CEILINGS ARE WHAT SEPARATE US FROM THE OUTSIDE WORLD. THEY ENCLOSE AND

DIVIDE OUR HOMES, MARKING OUT SHARED AND PRIVATE TERRITORY. MOST ARE SOLID, PROVIDING

A VISUAL AS WELL AS PHYSICAL DIVISION, BUT SLIDING PARTITIONS AND TRANSPARENT PANELS

MAKE AN INTERIOR LAYOUT MORE FLUID AND FLEXIBLE. USUALLY, SOLID SURFACES ARE DECORATED

WITH PAPER, FABRIC, OR PAINT, BUT TEXTURAL MATERIALS—WOOD, STONE, BRICK, AND

CONCRETE—CAN CREATE A SENSE OF PERMANENCE AND A RICHLY NEUTRAL BACKGROUND.

flexible space

Walls and ceilings define the spaces we live in, separating areas for different activities and allowing privacy where needed, but their solidity and permanence can sometimes be limiting. Employing translucent materials or movable partitions brings greater versatility.

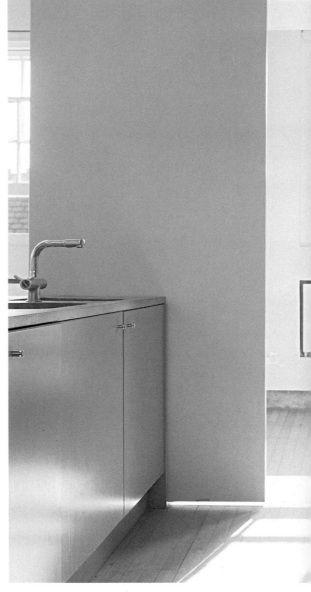

above **The sliding panels across one end of this kitchen can be opened to flood the room with daylight from the windows opposite or closed to conceal the clutter of cooking.**

above right **In a room with a high ceiling, a sleeping platform suspended from the rafters extends the living space vertically without losing the sense of openness at ground level. Stairs rising to the platform, and their flanking wall, partially separate the study and kitchen areas but, because the wall stops short of the ceiling, light from the skylight floods the whole space.**

left **Subterranean rooms are, by definition, dark, but the basement level of this apartment in a former printing factory has been opened up to daylight by enlarging the stairwell and constructing a wall of glass bricks between the bedroom and stairway. The Solaris bricks are ribbed to give privacy while allowing light through.**

Solid walls are necessary to support the structure of our homes, but perhaps we do not need as many as we think. Most internal partitions are there for demarcation, to separate conflicting activities, give privacy, or define territory. They help reduce the transmission of sound from one living space to another, and they provide a background against which to arrange furniture. However, they also block the passage of light and are sometimes more confining than we would like. Open-plan spaces, having few visual anchors, screens, or boundaries, present different challenges, requiring imaginative arrangement of furniture and possessions, neatness and, in a family home, harmony and cooperation.

Between these extremes, however, there are opportunities for devising a more flexible interior that puts space to good use and can be adapted to changing demands. Movable walls are an effective way to alter space for aesthetic or practical reasons. They neatly negotiate the limitations imposed by conventional walls by allowing the shape and character of a room to be changed without recourse to builders. In winter, spaces can be made smaller and more snug; in summer, the partitions open up to give an expansive, airy feel. Kitchens, dining rooms, studies, or halls can be screened off when contained spaces are required and opened up for extra space and a more convivial atmosphere. Such partitions can be as simple and temporary as a freestanding screen or a more permanent arrangement of folding doors or sliding panels.

Walls made from glass or other translucent materials may not physically enlarge a space, but by allowing light to pass into gloomy rooms, stairwells, and basements from the windows in adjoining rooms, they make more use of the existing area and give a feeling of openness. The ceiling presents another opportunity to open up space, and where there is no attic above, a large skylight will bathe the room beneath it in light, give an enhanced feeling of space and, after dark, a stunning view of the night sky.

far left top and center **Glass bricks form one side of this shower enclosure allowing light from the bathroom to pass through. Textured rather than clear bricks are used to camouflage the inevitable splash marks.**
far left below **A glass roof means this living area is light and bright all year round, and the hard shadows produced on sunny days endow the architecture and furnishings with a sculptural quality. Glazed roofs must be made from toughened (laminated) glass for safety and need easily operated opening devices for comfort.**
left **The bottom half of this wall is made from obscured glass bricks for privacy. The clear glass above offers a view of the trees, which provide shelter in summer and uninterrupted daylight in winter.**

right **In some situations, absolute transparency can be confusing and potentially hazardous. Here clear glass bricks allow views through the space, but the grid of joints between them indicates the presence of a wall.**
center right **Translucent glass panels enclose an area of privacy within an open-plan space without greatly reducing the natural light into the adjacent passageway.**
below, left and right **The wall beside this bathtub is made from Privalite electro-polarizing glass, which contains an interlay that changes from clear to opaque when the power is turned on. Expensive but effective, the glass can be left clear to give a feeling of space in the bathroom or switched on when privacy is required.**

glass

Glass blurs the boundaries of any living space, bringing the outside in or allowing light to spill from room to room.

The brilliance, clarity, and translucence of glass makes it a favorite material for modern interiors, where it enhances light and creates a feeling of spaciousness. Glass walls come in the form of bricks or panels, and may be textured to obscure the view without sacrificing light. For those who need transparency and privacy at different times, there is electrically controlled glass that can be switched from clear to cloudy.

stone, concrete, brick, & plaster

On the inside, the hard materials that form the fabric of a building are usually hidden from view, but when exposed, the most familiar of these can take on a decorative value in their own right.

While these hard surfaces, more usually concealed under layers of paint and wallpaper, undoubtedly add character and texture to a room, they are cold surfaces and need the contrast of warmer materials—in the form of furniture, fabrics, or other wall surfaces—to create a positive balance.

Stone, concrete, brick, and plaster each have a distinct personality, and they seem to divide conveniently into traditional and modern styles; but typecasting is dangerous. Of the four, concrete, a utilitarian material with industrial associations, is more likely to fit its style profile, being most suited to a stripped-back modern interior in a large urban space. The others have more chameleonlike qualities.

above left **The natural fissures that occur in creamy travertine marble give the stone texture and sophistication. It is available as wall panels from marble suppliers.**
above right **The walls of this converted industrial building in the north of England are built from the local gritstone, and have been repointed but are** otherwise untreated. **The stainless-steel hand rail and plate-steel staircase are stylistically appropriate.**
right **This wall has been stripped back to reveal the texture and mellow color of the bare brick. Old bricks are invariably dusty, but a broad dado of recycled lumber at the right height will protect passers-by from contact with the surface.**

left **The diagonal beams of this concrete ceiling were left exposed to show its structure and bear witness to the building's industrial origins. The surface was sealed against dust with clear adhesive, diluted to a consistency to be completely absorbed so as not to alter the appearance of the concrete.**

opposite, above left **This fireplace wall is built from Idaho quartzite honey ledgestone, which is indigenous to the locality. Laid in a random ashlar pattern with the grout joints raked deep, the arrangement of stones enhances the horizontal lines of the house.**

opposite, above right **The wall and ceiling here are lined with panels of cementitious fiberboard screwed to a wood and steel frame. Revealing elements of the building that are usually unseen gives the interior a raw, unrefined quality.**

opposite, below right **Exposing a brick wall is not simply a matter of hacking away old plaster. To remove surface dirt, the brickwork should be sand- or grit-blasted—a treatment which, in the case of this wall, softened the color to a warm honey tone.**

opposite, below center **Brickwork that is intended to be seen has an entirely different character to the kind that has been stripped of its plaster. Bright, regular, and well defined, it can play a leading role in a contemporary scheme alongside other well-groomed building materials such as concrete and wood.**

opposite, below left **This three-dimensional partition contains a shower and washbasin within its organic shape. A conventional stud construction was covered with flexible sheet fiberglass (instead of rigid wallboard) to form the smoothly curved ends. Its exterior is finished with Armourcoat Spatulata, a decorative, lightly textured finish that resembles Venetian plaster.**

Stone can be stately, elegant, rustic, or modern. Think of the perfectly dressed stone walls in the hall of a Federal townhouse and compare them with highly finished travertine in a modern bathroom, the rugged granite blocks of a rustic cottage, or evenly hewn stones used in a contemporary country home in the mountains. All are stone, but in style and presentation, are quite different.

Brick is equally versatile. The mellow tones and matte, powdery texture of age-worn brick makes it a sympathetic material for both traditional interiors and modern converted industrial spaces, while the bright, uniform color and regular shapes of new brick have a sleekness that blends well with other well-groomed contemporary surfaces like polished concrete and oiled hardwood.

Plaster is probably the latest material to be recognized for its decorative potential, but where it is left bare, it is rarely in its natural form. The new decorative plasterwork is more often a surface coating applied by specialists and polished, textured, or tinted to achieve finishes of considerable sophistication. Polished plaster has a chic, metropolitan look, while textured plaster gives an impression of age—if not antiquity—and, in neutral or warm earthy colors, is an ideal backdrop for antique or modern furniture.

this page, above **Veneers allow the natural grain of rare and exotic woods to be used decoratively over a large area.** These closets owe their unusual texture to sapele pomelle, a veneer cut from the root of the sapele—a wood sometimes referred to as African mahogany.

this page, center left **Rich brown iroko planks fitted horizontally to cover an entire wall are juxtaposed with a clear glass balustrade.** The choice of simple, if expensive, materials and the lack of any embellishment create an elegant background for classic contemporary furniture.

this page, center right **Fine materials like this burl-oak veneer are unusual in a kitchen, but the quality of the cabinetry forges a unity between this room and the adjoining, similarly luxurious dining room.**

this page, below **Wood paneling need not restrict your color scheme. Paint is a quick, simple and inexpensive way to change the look of the room without losing its intrinsic character.**

opposite, above left **In this converted oast house, built for the purpose of** drying hops, the original ceiling would have been slatted to allow heat to rise. The new slatted softwood ceiling, modeled on the old, has been stained to mimic the color of heat-darkened beams.

opposite, above right **This wooden ceiling is unusual in that the beams appear to run parallel with the rafters—an effect the architect used to emphasize the ceiling's direction and drama.** In fact, the wood in the ceiling is hemlock paneling, milled to replicate the width of the Douglas fir rafters and attached to the underside of the plywood roof decking that spans the rafters.

opposite, below left **Plywood may be an inexpensive material but, if skilfully installed, it has visual and practical integrity.** Here the boards are perfectly level, edges abutted with joints arranged in a regular staggered-brick pattern. Light reflecting off its golden surface casts a warm and flattering glow over the room.

opposite, below right **Recycled rafters supporting a steeply pitched roof accentuate its soaring height and add to its character.**

wood

One of the most ancient building materials, wood is warm, tactile, and responsive. It contributes greatly to the quality of our lives, bringing color, pattern, and a resinous perfume into our homes.

The clichéd view of wood walls and ceilings concerns oak beams and dark paneling, but wood comes in many varieties and offers unlimited decorative possibilities. In the hands of a craftsman, fine veneers cut from rare and exotic woods create luxurious interiors in the style of an ocean liner, while unremarkable lumber like softwood and plywood, used imaginatively, make interesting surfaces with or without the help of stains, seals, and lacquers.

top **A contemporary interpretation of the concept of wood paneling, this veneered wall is figured like the contours on a map, the flowing grain contained by leaving narrow spaces between the panels.**

above **Wood in a traditional setting: this oak partition wall conforms to the post-and-panel method of construction commonly used up to the 17th century, where planks or panels filled the spaces between wooden studs. The heavy central ceiling beam is one of the main supports for the building's upper story.**

right **Commonly used in early California Modern architecture, indigenous redwood, cut in broad 12 inch (30 cm) tongue-and-groove panels, covers the walls of this house. It has physical and visual warmth and, used indoors and out, helps blend the building with its natural surroundings.**

this page, top **Sometimes the only economical way to deal with a crumbling ceiling is to cover it up. In this hall, a virtue has been made of necessity by installing a decorative false ceiling. Painted dark red, it is strengthened by narrow beams in dark green to match the door frames, while rounded corner pieces complete the faux-gothic effect.**

this page, center **The division of walls into border, field, and dado was a classically inspired Georgian formula for decorating. Here the dado, including the chair rail and baseboard, is painted white in sparkling contrast with the deep red above.**

this page, below **Paneled walls denote tradition and formality, emphasize symmetry, and, in a large room, break up expanses of wall.**

opposite, top left and center **This fine wood paneling, painted a light putty color (OW17 by Papers and Paints), is an original feature of this 19th-century house. The lower part is relatively simple, but the deep carved border is a typically Aesthetic style.**

opposite, top right **This ceiling in the same house has carved wood crossribs in the vernacular style. The hanging light by 20th-century designer Serge Mouille is an unlikely but successful flourish.**

opposite, center left **First conceived to protect walls from being marked by furniture, wood-paneled dados now serve to improve the proportions of a room and give a sense of character and permanence.**

opposite, below left **Modern décor and traditional architecture can mix, provided each is awarded due respect. Here, no attempt is made to disguise the Victorian plasterwork ceiling—rather it is accentuated by painting the molding a stronger color.**

opposite, below right **Tongue-and-groove wainscoting is a serviceable wall treatment most often seen in country kitchens and other hard-working rooms. Here, newly installed tongue-and-groove lines the staircase leading to the basement kitchen of an 18th-century townhouse. An alcove set into the curved wall is a quirky touch.**

decorative details

Plain, smooth walls and ceilings are blank canvases inviting decoration, and there are limitless ways to embellish them. Surface decoration adds color and pattern, but plasterwork and paneling adds a third dimension and a sense of permanence.

People have embellished the walls of their homes from the earliest times, and it is an urge that evolution and civilization have never dimmed. A traditional way to decorate—and insulate—walls is with wood paneling. The 18th-century fashion for classical architecture led to a formula for positioning horizontal panel moldings to correspond with the proportions of the classical column. So, the baseboard represented the column base, the dado or chair rail the pedestal, and the ceiling molding the entablature. This formula survived, and though it is unusual to find rooms with full traditional wood paneling, a wood-paneled dado or at least a dado rail and baseboard is a familiar feature. The type of wood paneling found in period houses varies in quality and extravagance of design, depending on the status of the room. In family or servant's areas, tongue-and-groove wainscoting was the norm, but more extravagant paneling can be found in rooms used for entertaining. In older buildings, ceilings, too, are embellished. Usually the decoration is plasterwork molded in complex and elaborate designs, but elsewhere, beams and crossbeams form a rectangular grid across the surface.

Plain walls and ceilings are most often decorated with paint or wallpaper in styles that change with fashion. Currently flat paint is in vogue, but in past decades satin and gloss finishes have had their moments. Specialized paint finishes are favored by some as a way of adding pattern and texture to paintwork or producing faux finishes that mimic stone, marble, or another natural material. Glazes

left and top left **Leather panels, suspended from a ceiling-mounted track, form an effective partition. Made in the same way as a vertical louvered blind and operated by similar fixtures, the overlapping leather vanes appear as a solid partition but are slightly tilted to allow some light through while visually dividing the space. The panels were designed by Filer & Cox.**

above center, left and right **This wall, pierced with angular recesses in which to display beautifully shaped vessels, was built across an alcove to give the room a square, streamlined plan. The recesses are painted in neutral shades of gray, taupe, and chocolate brown, and lit from within.**

above right **The visible fibers in this Indian parchment paper from Bilhuber Basics, and the fact that it is hung in panels with visible seams instead of conventional drops, give a subtle texture that makes it difficult to discern whether it is indeed paper or some sophisticated stone finish.**

right **Op-art wallpaper designs need to be seen in their entirety to fully appreciate the illusory effect. This slightly three-dimensional paper is vintage, but similar designs can be found in current selections.**

far right, above and below **A discreet painted dado has been created by contrasting flat and reflective finishes. Set higher than usual at shoulder height, the dado has a stylized wave edge separating the pearlescent glaze below and the flat paint above.**

can be used to add pearly, metallic, or sparkling finishes to flat color to produce playful effects that are, tantalizingly, only apparent when they catch the light.

Wallpapers are an easy way to introduce color and pattern to a room. In addition to thousands of printed designs, there are many interesting textured papers to choose from. Embossed papers were once the most common type and are still widely available in traditional and abstract designs, but blown vinyl, a heat-expanded plastic material applied to the surface, provides the relief pattern on many modern papers. Random-textured papers have taken time to shrug off the legacy of cheap woodchip, but the newest ethnic or handmade-look papers are glamorous and sophisticated. Sometimes they come in small sheets, like wrapping paper, but accurately hung, with the seams staggered, the result can resemble ashlar stonework.

STAIRCASES

THE STAIRCASE COULD BE SEEN SIMPLY AS A FUNCTIONAL STRUCTURE, BUT BECAUSE IT OCCUPIES

SUCH A PROMINENT AND CENTRAL POSITION IN THE HOUSE, IT IS A MAJOR ARCHITECTURAL

FEATURE. IN TRADITIONAL HOUSES, THE STAIRCASE CAN BE AN ACCURATE INDICATOR OF PERIOD,

BUT IN CONTEMPORARY BUILDINGS, NO SUCH RULES APPLY, AND IT CAN BE ENCLOSED IN A

STAIRWELL OR OPEN PLAN, STRAIGHT OR SPIRAL, AND MADE FROM VIRTUALLY ANY MATERIAL

THAT IS SAFE AND STRONG ENOUGH FOR THE PURPOSE.

spatial flow

There's an argument for nominating the staircase as the focus of the home. It is often the first thing you see when you enter the house; it occupies a central position, and it connects every level. The first flight of a staircase is invariably the most impressive because it is a key feature of the entrance hall, and its style, whether traditional or modern, can set the tone for the design of the rest of the house.

The staircase is not just a functional structure giving access to the different floors in a house, it is also an important design feature right at its heart and exerts a powerful influence over the areas surrounding it Traditional staircases made from wood are bulky and occupy a large amount of space. The best of them are beautifully constructed with carved or turned newel posts, sweeping handrails and slow curves that carry the eye upward. The worst are narrow, poorly lit, sharply angled and badly positioned.

Replacing a less-than-lovely staircase for something more aesthetically pleasing can improve an interior dramatically by making better use of space and by reducing the substance of the staircase to allow more light to pass through. However, the project will be expensive and disruptive, and should not be undertaken without professional help and a clear set of objectives. Heritage-building owners need special permission to carry out major changes of this kind, and anyone thinking of installing a new staircase must be aware

above **This centrally positioned staircase is designed as an atrium, naturally lit from a large skylight above and enclosed by glass walls so light passes into the surrounding rooms.**
right **A conventional staircase made from glass gives the very unconventional effect of a light well cutting through all levels of a house.**
opposite **In a spacious loft apartment, a sinuous modern staircase curves around the architecture. It is a dramatic feature, but because of its light frame, does not dominate.**

of any regulations that might stipulate requirements for the pitch of the stairs, the amount of headroom, and the design of the banisters.

If your main aim is to reduce the amount of space taken up by the staircase, a spiral design is a possible solution, but bear in mind that it will be difficult to carry large pieces of furniture up and down it, and you will lose much useable understairs space. Custommade spirals are often dramatically sculptural and would have a strong presence in an entrance hall, but those bought as standard readymades are perhaps better suited for linking upper storys. If your hope is to make better use of the surrounding space in the hall or landing, the staircase may be repositioned to facilitate

this, but if it is important to create a more contemporary look and a sense of space at the center of your home, a staircase with an open construction, flooded with natural light, is the answer.

One of the most successful ways of drawing light into a staircase is to install a large skylight directly above it. If the staircase has a fine enough framework and is built from translucent materials, the light will pass unhindered through the stairwell, making the whole house seem brighter and more spacious. For a project like this, the likelihood is that the staircase will have to be custom-made, but by working closely with an architect or designer, the result will be a unique centerpiece to your home.

right **In this house, a contemporary interpretation of the 1930s Moderne style, the staircase typically rises from the living area to open up the space. Open treads and a geometric metal-and-glass balustrade add to the feeling of spaciousness, and the effect is enhanced by daylight streaming down from the rooflight overhead.**

below **Curved walls, exposed, gray-painted metalwork, and porthole lights give this open-plan interior a nautical atmosphere, which is added to by the spiral staircase leading to an open, decklike landing. Made from a combination of silvery gray metal and light wood, the stairs seem more an integral part of the structure than simply a means of moving from one level to another.**

opposite, left and right **Winding around the perimeter of a sky-lit atrium at the center of a tall, narrow townhouse, this staircase is a bright space in daylight hours. The glass walls separating the staircase from the surrounding rooms are translucent where privacy is needed and clear where a feeling of space is the priority, but the result is always the same—to double the volume of light flowing through the interior.**

right, above and below **It is hard to believe that this imposing staircase at the heart of an early-19th-century townhouse is less than ten years old. Made to order, it fits the house perfectly, following the austerely elegant late Georgian style of plain square-section balusters set two to a tread with a sinuous, slim mahogany handrail. Winding through the heart of the house, it sweeps in generous curves from the center of the ground floor to the upper levels and down around a wide stairwell to the basement, encouraging the free flow of light and activity.**
opposite, left **A straight flight of wooden steps may be the most functional of staircases, but this one, made from beautifully grained wood, demonstrates how quality of materials and manufacture can elevate a plain design to classic status. Most stairs form the focus of an entrance hall, but in this house where the steep downward slope of the site makes it more practical to site the bedrooms on a lower level than the living area, the staircase leading to them is more discreet.**
opposite, right **A staircase across the center of a studio apartment may seem like an inefficient use of space, but here, with a short flanking wall, it forms a division between the kitchen and office. The understairs cavity, accessed from the kitchen side, provides housing for appliances. In this predominantly white space, hard maple, a pale and durable wood, faces the treads and risers, bringing definition to the shape of the staircase.**
below left **Open-tread wooden steps cantilevered from a wood-paneled wall recede into their background. The open ends of the steps are linked in pairs by chrome bolts that also serve to warn of the projecting edges.**
below right **In an apartment divided into interlocking spaces, this enclosed staircase leads to a mezzanine library at one end of the tall living room. Glass circles set into the staircase wall allow light from an entrance hall, tucked under the mezzanine, to illuminate the stairs.**

wooden stairs

Traditional stairs are constructed almost entirely from wood, from the unseen structural parts to the carved decoration, but modern staircases made primarily from harder materials often use wooden handrails and treads to add a warm and tactile element.

Wood is probably the ideal material for a staircase. In construction, it is strong and easy to work; decoratively, it is sympathetic and versatile. It lends itself to traditional and modern styles, and can be stained, polished, painted, or carpeted when a new look is required. Traditional stairs are likely to be more substantial, with rounded stair nosings,

turned balusters, and carved newel posts. Modern wooden stairs are pared-down and may consist of nothing more than a series of open treads cantilevered from a wall or wooden facings covering a flight of concrete steps. Where traditional stairs rely on decorative detailing, modern ones let the color and grain of the wood speak for itself.

glass & metal

For some, climbing a glass staircase is like taking a step into the unknown, but what transparent stairs lack in visual substance they more than make up for in glamour. Seen in fashionable restaurants and stylish office buildings, glass is quickly being accepted as a material for stairs in innovative domestic interiors. Metal stairs, too, are making the move from public to private spaces. Valued for its strength without bulk, metal has become the material of choice for designers of light, open staircases.

Conventional staircases are large, solid structures that occupy considerable space at the center of a house, blocking the flow of light from the front to the back of the building. Open-tread stairs and fine balusters, in particular the lightness of metal structures, allow some light to penetrate the mass, but transparent and reflective glass stairs allow the free passage of light throughout the space.

Glass—brittle, delicate, easily broken—may seem an unsuitable material for stairs, but put aside thoughts of fragile windowpanes and wineglasses, and consider instead the resilient glass of car windshields and store windows. The glass used for stair treads is composed of two or three layers laminated together. The total thickness depends on the size of the tread and the weight it is expected to carry, but in a home staircase 1¼–2 inches (32–50 mm) is the norm. The glass may be water-clear, colored, or textured and, for safety, should be etched to prevent the surface from being too slippery. An alternative material is acrylic. It is virtually identical in appearance to clear glass, but easier to work with since it can be cut, machined, and drilled into without breaking. Its disadvantages are that the surface will scratch, and as the material is flammable, it should not be used for a staircase that will be an escape route in a fire.

Metal stairs, straight or spiral, can be made with a structure so fine that light appears to pass through unobstructed, an effect that is enhanced if the metal used is polished. Open treads with pierced surfaces combine with balustrades filled with clear glass or acrylic panels, wire mesh, or tension wires to increase the ratio of space to structure and give a greater impression of openness without losing any sense of security for those using the stairs.

opposite, above **A narrow, enclosed staircase always has the makings of a dark and gloomy place reliant on artificial light, but here, open-tread semi-opaque glass steps allow natural light from above and below to flood through the space. The steps, slightly narrower than the staircase width, are discreetly bolted to the flanking walls, giving them the appearance of floating in space.**

opposite, below **This staircase, leading from a large, sparsely furnished living space to a gallery bedroom, is skeletal in design. Supported on a light framework of black metal, it has slim white laminated treads and a tubular brushed-steel handrail.**

this page **Architect Alan Power designed this glass staircase contained behind a glass wall as part of a radical remodel of a Georgian rowhouse. Extending the full three storys of the building, the transparent structure allows a skylight at the top to illuminate the open-plan living areas. The toughened glass and acrylic laminated treads rest on stainless-steel shoes, bolted on one side to a steel stringer concealed in the solid party wall and on the other to the triple-laminated glass staircase wall. When the treads are backlit by a sun low in the sky, their front edges glow luminous blue-green. To help define the steps and make them slip-resistant, a dotted border has been etched along the front of each tread.**

83

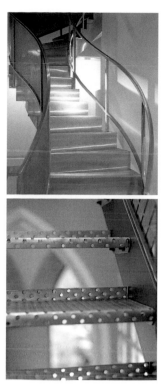

opposite and above left **This sculptural staircase by VX Design and Architecture is a dark and dramatic feature in a light open-plan living space. In reverse of convention, the space below the stairs is open, and the space above is enclosed by a welded rolled-steel plate suspended from the structural steel of the upper floor. The stair treads are made of ½ inch (15 mm) frosted glass held in bottomless welded metal trays. These are fixed to the notched lower edge of the steel plate at one side and to a steel stringer, concealed in the wall, at the other. Although the overall impression is dark, the staircase receives daylight from above and from the underside via the glass treads and open risers.**

above center top **A large staircase can easily overwhelm a space, but the flowing shape and reflective surfaces of this one** create a stream of light at the center of a large, open living area. Unusually, the steps are covered in a continuous sheet of aluminum, like a metal carpet, and top-lit by halogen spotlights to shimmering effect.

above center bottom **Pierced metal stair treads have enough texture to provide a reassuring grip and the right balance of solidity and openness. This industrial-style staircase, with balustrades made from glass and black mesh, links the living areas in a converted church without restricting the flow of light. When light catches the metal, surrounding surfaces are peppered with pinpricks of light.**

above right **This spiral staircase appears to provide an interior link between a dining room and an upper floor, but it actually gives external access to a roof terrace. The confusion arises because the clear glass stairwell** surrounding the outdoor stairway encroaches into the rectangular interior plan.

center right **Curving out and up, this open-tread metal staircase follows the rounded wall of a converted British "oast" house, starting at a gentle climb but rising more steeply toward the top. The simple balustrade repeats the curve, but does not detract from it, the space between the handrail and treads being filled unobtrusively with tension wires.**

below right **An open mesh of wire within a tubular metal frame surrounds this stairwell, providing safety without enclosing or over-shadowing the space. Although the components are relatively inexpensive and the installation simple, the balustrade has a pleasingly functional quality that is not out of place in this home setting.**

stone & concrete

Staircases made from stone or concrete have a reassuring solidity underfoot and an unrivaled sense of permanence. Often integral to the design of the building, they are an acute indicator of its style.

Stone or concrete steps can be a permanent reminder of a building's origins. A sweeping stone staircase in an 18th-century house gives an air of grandeur, while concrete steps in a converted commercial building give a clue to its industrial beginnings. In contemporary homes, stone stairs are often more of a decorative statement than an architectural one, with an existing staircase and hallway surfaced with stone tiles or panels. Concrete forms a good base for this treatment, but wooden stairs, provided they are sound and have been leveled with a covering of marine plywood, can be successfully stone clad.

far left **White precast concrete steps fan out from the central pillar of this spiral stairway, extending the height of the building. The steps end about 4 inches (100 mm) short of the curved stairwell wall, and although there is limited visibility from the staircase to the floors it links, the perimeter gap allows the passage of sound and light** from level to level, making this a true connecting space.

center, above and below **In this contemporary home, the stairs and landing floor are clad with the same dark "mussel" limestone, but an impression of contrast is created by the way light strikes the horizontal and vertical surfaces. On the stair risers, the color and pattern** of the stone is very evident, but on the horizontal surfaces of the treads and landing area, the gleaming polished finish dominates.

above **The white-painted walls, glass brick panels, honey-colored wooden handrail, and slate-covered steps combine in this staircase to create a cool, quiet oasis at the heart of the building.**

HEATING

DESPITE ADVANCES IN HEATING TECHNOLOGY THAT GIVE WARMTH WITHOUT A VISIBLE SOURCE OF HEAT, IN COLDER CLIMES THE HEARTH CONTINUES TO BE A FOCUS IN MANY HOMES. OPEN FIREPLACES COME IN AN EVER-WIDENING RANGE TO SUIT TRADITIONAL AND MODERN INTERIORS, WHILE RADIATORS, NO LONGER IN THE BACKGROUND, COME IN PERIOD STYLES AND SCULPTURAL CONTEMPORARY SHAPES.

right **This simple white limestone fireplace, made to order, is framed with a traditional bolection molding and contains Gazco's simple Amhurst steel grate.**

opposite, above left **An essay in understatement, this fireplace is made from Bath stone, just a shade darker than the wall.**

opposite, above right **A pared-down version of a traditional design, this fireplace is decorated with just three roundels spaced evenly across the frieze. It was made to order by a stone mason from a finely veined misty white Carrara marble.**

opposite, below left **With its outlined columns and black stars, this limestone fireplace is influenced by Empire style. Made to order by Chesney's, it is an adaptation of the company's Thomas Hope surround and contains a Wentworth register grate.**

opposite, below center **The fireplace and television often compete as a focal position, but when turned off, both leave a blank space at the center of the room. Here, they are set one above the other—a fan-assisted flue eliminating the need for a conventional chimney. When not in use, a large track-mounted painting slides across to conceal them. The satin stainless-steel fire is designed by MOOArc. The picture slides on a track made by Widney.**

opposite, below right **This chimneypiece designed by IPL Interiors, made from pale limestone, has at its center contemporary patinated bronze "Petra" andirons by Garouste & Bonetti flanking a natural-gas "log" fire.**

fireplaces

Warming, inviting, and visually magnetic, in cooler climates the fireplace is the natural center of a living room. It is part of the architecture, and whether original to the building or newly installed, its style sets the tone for the room.

Now that homes can be heated cleanly and efficiently from an unseen source, it seems odd that the fireplace still survives, but the warmth, color, and movement of an open fire hold an irresistible attraction that makes it a natural focus. The presence of a fireplace is unsurprising in an older house, where it is a vital part of the architecture and character of a room, but many new homes are built with a hearth in the living room, and modern fireplace design is a growth industry.

Classic fireplaces are composed of a surround or chimneypiece framing the fire opening, a grate where the fuel burns, and a hearth to protect the floor from ash and embers. The surround is usually made from marble, natural or reconstituted stone, metal, or wood, in a size and style to suit the room. The grate may consist of andirons to support logs, a fire-basket for logs or solid fuel, or a register grate—a unit made entirely of metal or with tiled panels, which fills the fireplace opening and is designed for the efficient burning of coal or smokeless fuel. If you want the look of a real fire without the inconvenience of storing fuel and cleaning the grate, fire-baskets and register grates can be equiped with gas-fueled flame-effect units or less convincing electric models. Readymade

opposite and above **An inset fire built into the chimneybreast fits flush to the wall and occupies no floor space A focal point, but never intrusive, it is the ultimate minimalist fireplace. Designed by Unique Environments for a contemporary interior, this fire is made from black metal. The fire-bed is composed of matte white pebbles of various sizes which look natural but are actually ceramic. Unlike real stone, ceramic is resistant to very high temperatures and will not discolor with heat.**

above right **A "black box" inset fire seems less cavernous, thanks to the reflective bronze Japanese paper covering the wall, which shimmers even when the fire is not lit.**

right **An old stone fireplace is an appropriate choice for this basement family room, which must once have been the staff quarters of this 19th-century townhouse. Bought from a salvage yard, it was originally much wider than required, but a "cut-and-shut" operation to remove the excess width from the center maintained its symmetry.**

fireplaces in modern, classic, and traditional styles are widely available. However, if you are after a custommade design, these can be commissioned from specialized workshops or craftsmen, and period pieces can be found in architectural salvage yards.

The newest kind of open fire, designed for contemporary interiors, is the inset or hole-in-the-wall type. Stripped of the inessentials, they have no surround or mantelshelf, and are simply a fire opening set in the wall with a conventional fire-basket or a gas-fueled fire-bed of pebbles, rocks, synthetic logs, or ceramic shapes. Unless they are protected by a glass or metal mesh screen at the front, for safety, inset fires should have a projecting hearth on the floor below or as part of the fire itself.

left **Although the hearth itself is small, the magnificent copper hood above it transforms this fireplace into the central feature of an Arts and Crafts interior. Such a distinctive fireplace would have been designed—and preserved—as an integral part of the building, but occasionally salvaged fireplaces are sold by dealers specializing in the style.**

below far left **A chimneypiece that is wider than it is high has a generous, expansive feel. Its proportions are unusual, but the exaggerated width of this fireplace has an elegance in keeping with the understated traditional American interior. The large hearth is amply filled by a pair of typically Federal turned brass-and-iron andirons.**

below near left **The rugged boulder that forms the lintel over this stone fireplace has survived from the remains of the previous house to occupy this site. A similar fireplace could be constructed from roughhewn stone bought direct from a quarry or via a stonemason.**

opposite **Part of the original carved wood panelling in an Aesthetic-Movement house, this chimneypiece has been painted a light putty color to reduce its visual weight without detracting from the carved decoration.**

above left **Commissioned for a house built in the 1940s in the Arts and Crafts style, this craftsman-made repoussé brass surround frames a trapezoid fireplace opening. While the choice of metal leans toward Arts and Crafts, its angular, asymmetrical design shows distinct Modernist influences.**
below left **In its original state, this Victorian fireplace would have had a white marble surround and patterned tiled panels in the register grate. By painting the surround a warm shade of taupe and replacing the** tiles with plain cream ones, the period detail is toned down and the fireplace blends more comfortably with the eclectic style of its surroundings.
center **A traditional Victorian fireplace assumes a much more exotic image at the center of a room decorated in red and black. The cast-iron surround could have been shot-blasted to give a dark gunmetal gray finish, but where an opaque, nonmetallic black is required, paint is the answer. Touches of gold paint highlight the relief decoration in the fireplace frieze and echo gold** accents elsewhere in the room.
above There are differing schools of thought about original architectural features. One is that they should be preserved at all costs; the other is that they reflect the fashions of the past and should be altered or replaced when tastes change. A third, more cautious view is that they can be integrated into a new style of decoration. Here, this cautious approach works successfully as the fireplace, painted the same color as the wall, is a significant feature but not a dominating one.

radiators

Central heating is generally provided, behind the scenes, by forced-air systems, but in some situations, radiators provide the look desired. Happily, there are models to suit most tastes.

Where once ridged panels hung in the middle of a wall, sometimes even painted to contrast with the surface behind them, now heating is increasingly discreet. Radiators are hidden behind paneling or in a trench, with only a neat grille to indicate their presence. Where they are exposed, radiators are chosen for their inconspicuous styling and ability to blend into surroundings or because their design adds to the overall look of the space they heat.

Radiators must have space around them to allow the heat to circulate, so to a degree they determine the arrangement of furniture in a room. However, they can be made to slot

above far left Least obtrusive of all radiators, trench heaters, produced by companies such as Jaga, are sunk into the ground and covered with a grille flush to the floor. Because they are so well insulated, any type of flooring can be used around them.

above center left Chosen for its workmanlike appearance and its high heat output in relation to its compact shape, this finned tubular radiator by Gunning Engineering in one of four heating a large studio apartment in a converted industrial building.

above center right Boxed-in radiators look best when they are part of the architecture, and here the radiator cover fills the window alcove. A long grille set into the top of the cabinet allows rising heat to escape, warming the cold area close to the glass.

above near left Traditional column radiators assume a contemporary look when they are much taller than they are wide. A number of manufacturers make the columns individually, so while there is a range of standard heights, almost any width can be achieved.

below far left The designer of this all-white hall chose a Zehnder panel radiator for its low visual input and high heat output. Virtually uncontoured, with its fine horizontal seams casting minimal shadows, the panel seems to disappear into the wall behind.

below center The Zehnder Radiavector is one of the few radiators shallow enough to fit under a window as low as this without obscuring the glass. A double convector radiator, it efficiently counteracts the cooling effect of the uncurtained window.

below near left In a bathroom, where space is often limited, a radiator that is part-heater, part-towel rod, like those from the Ecotherm line by Thermic, earns the space it occupies. The wide spaces between rails allow for bulky towels, but some rails must be left uncovered to allow heat into the room.

above left **Slim and unobtrusive, this panel heater is set into an alcove where its surface is unlikely to come into accidental contact with bare skin. A rail fitted above allows towels to dry quickly and keep warm without blocking heat from the room.**

above **Traditional column radiators come in sizes to fit almost any situation. They can even be shaped to fit a curved wall. This wall-mounted example is the Multicolumn by Zehnder, and can be stove-enameled in a range of colors.**

left **A radiator cover hides an ugly radiator and integrates it in the room. This painted wood cabinet designed by IPL Interiors has a limestone shelf cut into the window embrasure to give an immaculately tailored fit.**

opposite, above left **If you buy salvaged radiators, make sure they have been refurbished. This** floor-standing cast-iron radiator has been shot-blasted to clean away old paint and chemically flushed to remove silt and corrosion from inside.

opposite, above right **A radiator's heat output is related to its surface area, so a long, low radiator gives as much warmth as a narrower taller one. This squat column radiator by Clyde Combustions is covered with a thick wooden bench to give it a more contemporary look and to help prevent rising heat from escaping through the window.**

opposite, below **It is hard to find the right reclaimed fixtures when you want them, so if you see something you like, buy it and wait for an opportunity to use it. These matching short radiators were a salvage-yard impulse buy, but installed side by side they make a stronger visual feature than a single long radiator.**

snugly into restricted spaces—long and low to fit under a large window or tall and slim to fill an alcove or the narrow space between two doors—thus allowing more flexibility. Debate continues about the advisability of positioning radiators under windows. While some heat will be lost through the glass, what is often a chilly part of the room will be made warmer and more usable. In bathrooms, towel radiators with horizontal rails are a practical option as they dry towels while they heat the room.

As radiators are semi-permanent fixtures, it is important to select a design that is compatible with your personal furnishing style and the style of the building. Period-house-dwellers after a traditional look have the choice of buying reproduction column radiators or hunting down suitable vintage ones in salvage yards. Column radiators are usually produced in sections, so can be made to the length required. Modern streamlined panels and sculptural feature radiators are available for contemporary interiors, and models that were designed for use in industrial settings are now available to those who live in converted commercial buildings. New radiators are usually primed and ready for painting, but increasingly they can be supplied with a more durable factory-applied coating in a choice of standard colors or metallic and customized finishes.

stoves

Undoubtedly cleaner and more efficient than an open fire, the workmanlike stove can heat soup, supply radiators with steam, and boil water, as well as providing direct warmth and a visual focus, whether it is on or off.

Above all, stoves are infinitely versatile. They can stand in the hearth like a conventional fire, flames flickering visibly through the glass-paneled doors, or in the middle of a room radiating controllable heat. They can be powered by solid fuel, wood, oil, natural gas, or electricity and have a predictable heat output measured in kilowatts. Although they still have a rustic image, styles range from basic pot-bellied and box stoves, through flat-black or colorful enameled traditional designs, to decorative reproduction Art Nouveau styles, and extremely stylish contemporary examples.

above **Cylinder stoves are ideal for small spaces like this converted railroad car as they occupy the minimum of floor space. Although this Summerford model was made only a few years ago it is no longer in production, but similar stoves are available.**

right **A high-output stove with an interior flue produces enough heat to give background warmth for this open-plan house. The Vermont Castings Defiant is similar to this double-door wood-burning stove and comes in colored enamel finishes as well as flat black.**

opposite, above left **This antique wood-burning stove was designed with safety in mind: a rail at the front prevents logs from falling out and clothing from catching the flames.**

opposite, above right **Box stoves are simple fuel burners: basic, inexpensive and sometimes even portable. Stoves similar to this were taken on early polar expeditions and are still used in country cabins and on houseboats. This plain design is an antique Shaker stove, but similarly functional models are available new.**

opposite, below left **Stoves are not always rustic or traditional, and many will sit comfortably in a modern setting. The Danish Rais 86 wood-burning stove, designed by Bent Falk in 1970, is a contemporary classic. A wide cylinder with a compartment below the firebox for storing wood and another above it with a soapstone plate for baking, the stove can heat a large living space.**

opposite, below right **Many European stove producers have been manufacturing for generations, and although new models are introduced from time to time, the design process is more often one of evolution. This traditional Scandinavian multifuel stove, made by Morsø, is an earlier version of its current Lion Radiant stove.**

STORAGE

WELL-PLANNED STORAGE BRINGS ORDER AND A SENSE OF SPACIOUSNESS TO ANY INTERIOR,

HOWEVER SMALL, LEAVING MORE ROOM TO DISPLAY FAVORITE THINGS. PURPOSE-MADE UNITS

FOR LIVING ROOMS AND BEDROOMS COME IN CHIC BUT FUNCTIONAL DESIGNS THAT CONTRIBUTE

TO THE STYLE OF THE ROOM, AND CLOSETS, TAILORED TO MAKE EFFICIENT USE OF LIMITED SPACE,

CAN BE SO CLEVERLY CONCEALED THAT YOU BARELY KNOW THEY ARE THERE.

left **Bookshelves tailored to fit under the eaves of an attic room make use of an under-employed space and provide a windowsill to display objects.**

below left **Designed in the 1980s by Vicent Martínez, the Literatura by Punt is a double bookcase with narrow shelves at the front which slide on tracks to reveal the continuous shelves behind.**

below **A wall of shelving is a practical way to provide a great deal of storage. This design by Bataille & ibens has sliding doors made from white Colorbel color-enameled glass by Glaverbel. They cover the lower part and hide the bar, stereo system, television, and the entrance to the adjoining laundry room. A wheeled ladder allows access to the higher shelves.**

right **Chosen to house an extensive art library, this Studimo shelving system by Interlübke is arranged here on two levels, the upper level being reached by a separate staircase. The shelves form a regular grid to accept books of any size so the collection can be catalogued without restriction.**

living rooms

Here storage needs to show off and enhance your favorite possessions, as well as look good in its own right.

The living room is where we gather around us the things we enjoy. It is here we read, listen to music, watch television, or spend time with friends and family, and it is here, too, that we keep the books, magazines, videos, DVDs, CDs, games, musical instruments, and other possessions that are the equipment of relaxation. These things reflect our interests, and by displaying them, we stamp our personality on the room.

above far left and left **A classic 1960s design by Dieter Rams, the 606 Universal shelving system from Vitsoe has adjustable powder-coated steel shelves and wood-and-aluminum drawers. It can be floor-standing, compressed between the floor and ceiling, or wall mounted as it is here.**
center far left and left **These custommade cubes designed to hold CDs, DVDs, and videos are made from lacquered composite board and have push catches so there are no handles to interrupt their clean lines. Mounted on a flat wall, they have a sculptural quality. Hung within an alcove, they appear sleekly built in. The shelf above the alcove cabinets is made of cast concrete.**
below far left **This built-in unit is one of a pair in the alcoves on each side of a chimneybreast. Designed in a simplified traditional style with molding and stylized pilasters, it has shelves above for display and cabinets below for hidden storage.**
below left **In a contemporary arrangement, open shelves are punctuated by painted closed compartments that hold less decorative clutter. The compartments effectively partition the shelves so books and objects can be displayed separately.**

above **These recessed shelves, tapered to fill the space under the stairs, are plastered and painted to appear as an integral part of the wall. Divided horizontally and vertically, they form niches in which to display favorite objects.**

left **A false wall built across one end of this dining room creates a substantial volume of storage. The space within is divided into two cupboards, and a pair of maple-framed sandblasted glass doors maintain symmetry.**

Different things require different types of storage. Books, especially if they form a substantial library, need sturdy shelving, and many of the best readymade modular systems have become design classics. CDs and DVDs, too, can be packed on shelves, but some individual objects, such as a piece of studio glass or a handmade ceramic bowl, whose prime purpose is to give visual pleasure, need space around them to be seen and appreciated. Where storage must be confined to one area—filling an alcove or covering a wall—shelves can be compartmentalized with vertical partitions to allow books and objects to be displayed together without encroaching on each other's space. In the interest of neatness or safekeeping, some possessions are best stored in containers, and most systems allow for this by incorporating drawers or closed cupboards. Where they do not, baskets or boxes can be placed on open shelves as a simple and inexpensive alternative.

bedrooms

The volume of things kept in a bedroom means that storage is as much a part of the décor as it is practical, making storage units central to the style of the room. Built-in closets are often the best solution, and simple designs will recede to become an integral part of the room and a neutral background for other furniture.

Clothes need careful storage. They must be easy to find and come out of the closet fresh, unrumpled, and ready to wear. They need space to hang freely; and folded garments should be stacked, uncrushed, in piles of two or three in shallow drawers or shelves. Shoe racks or pigeon-holes neatly sidestep the confusion of shoes found at the bottom of so many closets, and small drawers (or partitions in larger ones) keep smaller items in order.

above far left and left **So plain it could be mistaken for wood paneling, this custommade birch-veneer closet opens to reveal a meticulously planned interior. Rods are set in two tiers to make the best use of space, with a separate rod for shirts. The remaining space is devoted to drawers and pigeon-holes. An interior light makes it easy to see everything.**
left **In the same room, the paneling theme continues with a headboard and integrated nightstands in maple-edged birch veneer. The wall sconces are by Christian Liagre.**
above **Some furniture includes places to keep makeup, scarves, and accessories in order, but drawer dividers can be bought separately to organize interior space.**
opposite, above left and center left **The next best thing to a walk-in closet, this capacious armoire opens up to give a view of the entire contents. When closed, it blends into its white-painted surroundings.**
opposite, above right **Shallow drawers hold shirts without crushing them, and glass fronts allow you to find the one you want.**
opposite, below left **A filing system for clothes—small drawers keep individual garments immaculate and sloping pigeon-holes store shoes.**
opposite, below right **A sophisticated solution to clothes storage, this oak-lined Cuban mahogany closet wraps around one end of the dressing area off a master bedroom. Slim stainless-steel handles emphasize the height of the doors.**

work & leisure

Clutter is bad for you. It distracts you while you work and makes you restless when you want to relax. Ruthlessly clearing out possessions is one solution, but there will be things you can't or don't want to dispose of, and for these you need well-organized, good-looking storage.

Two major clutter-creating areas of your home are the office or work space, and the viewing and listening area. Technology promised to simplify storage in these areas, as computers, mini disks, and DVDs packed more information into a smaller space. In reality, the paperless office is still a distant dream; music and video collections expand to overflow the available space; and housing electronic hardware is complicated by changing formats as hi-fis become smaller, TVs larger, and home offices better equipped. Tackle these issues by providing shelves for the things you want to keep in view and cabinets for those you don't.

this page **Where a wall of tall storage might seem to enclose the room, these custom-built cabinets end at shoulder height, leaving space above for displaying pictures. Sliding doors can be opened easily in this confined space. In the upper section, these are made from frosted glass that can be drawn aside to reveal either the television screen or the decorative objects that stand alongside it.**

opposite, above left **Designed to fill the whole wall from floor to ceiling, this built-in storage system contains videos, tapes, disks, and all the other paraphernalia of home life behind closed doors, with only a wall-mounted CD player visible. Electronic controls allow the door concealing the television to be opened from the comfort of the sofa.**

opposite, center left **A narrow aluminum-front shelf suspended below wall-mounted cabinets contains hi-fi components. Ranged side by side, they appear to occupy less space than they would stacked vertically. The usual messy trail of cords is eliminated by the use of wireless speakers.**

opposite, below left **Complete in a colorful freestanding unit designed by Christian Biecher, this capsule home office keeps everything within easy reach.**

opposite, above right **When space and budget are limited, a simple do-it-yourself solution can work as well as sophisticated purpose-made furniture. Here, a galvanized-steel shelf unit becomes an ad hoc computer desk screened from the rest of the room—but not from the light—by a translucent clear plastic screen in a dark wood frame.**

opposite, below right **Carefully tailored to house the television, hi-fi, speakers, and a Linn system that provides music for the rest of the house, this storage system is built from composite board spray-painted in metallic dark gray lacquer, with door panels of stretched speaker fabric. Designed with an eye to the future, it has enough shelving to accommodate a fast-growing music collection.**

opposite **A row of tall cabinets in a passageway adjoining a kitchen and family room has the capacity to hold everything from dishes to craft materials, leaving the living space uncluttered. Independent but matching, the cabinets have a simplicity of design that does not detract from the vaulted ceiling.**

above left **A wall of bookshelves would not shave more than 12 inches (30 cm) from the width of a hall or landing, so in all but the narrowest spaces, a hall library is a practical proposition. Here, the book-lined passage houses the overspill from the study beyond and is wide enough to have a seat for browsing in comfort.**

above center **A similar treatment for a passageway linking two rooms, but this time storage is** behind the closed doors of low cabinets and the shelf space above is lit to give an impression of greater space at eye level.

above right **The smallest and most awkward spaces can be turned into useful storage. Here, a tiny cupboard has been squeezed into the narrow alcove beneath a window and next to a built-in settle. Ending short of the windowsill, its top forms a shelf.**

left **Built at the edge of an open-plan mezzanine bedroom, this painted armoire doubles as a screen between the bed and the floor below.**

below left **A series of built-in cabinets rises in tiers to fill a whole wall. Arranged in order of decreasing size, the largest are at floor level to give easy access to bulky items in frequent use, like the stroller.**

halls

The entrance hall may have its own storage needs, but landings and other through routes can provide a permanent home for things that have nowhere else to go.

Passageways and corridors are necessary but largely wasted spaces. They allow you to move around your home without passing from room to room, but most of the time they stand empty. If width allows, one or both walls of a hall or landing may have shelves or cupboards, and in smaller, awkwardly shaped spaces, an attractive piece of storage furniture will hold your possessions and look good.

LIGHTING

GOOD LIGHTING BRINGS A ROOM TO LIFE, CREATING ATMOSPHERE, HIGHLIGHTING POINTS OF INTEREST, AND ENHANCING THE COLORS AND TEXTURES OF FURNISHINGS. TO ACHIEVE THE MOST INTERESTING EFFECTS, COMBINE FIXTURES THAT GIVE BRIGHT DIRECT LIGHT, SOFT DIFFUSED ILLUMINATION, AND WARM BACKGROUND LIGHT WITH DECORATIVE FREESTANDING LAMPS, THEN ADD DIMMER CONTROLS TO FINE-TUNE THE RESULT.

information & decoration

Electric lights replace daylight after dark and supplement it when natural light is insufficient, but the fact that they are necessary is no reason for them to be purely functional. A powerful decorating tool, lighting can enhance or subdue colors, flatter or play down objects and architectural features, and subtly indicate the layout of your space.

Every interior needs general illumination, but it is the additional lighting that, by drawing attention to the features and hazards in our homes, makes them attractive, convenient and safe to live in. Information lighting is one of the most practical examples of lighting for emphasis, and might take the form of an exterior light above the front door or lights recessed into the floor along a windowless hallway. Decorative emphasis is provided in many ways. A spotlight that highlights a piece of furniture, a floodlight that accentuates the size and openness of an interior space, wall lamps that emphasize the texture or color of a wall, concealed lights that suggest mystery—all play their part in creating visual interest.

top left **Paper, parchment, and natural textiles make excellent materials for lampshades because they conceal the light source while allowing softened, diffused light to pass through. Choose a bulb of not more than 60 watts to avoid scorching the material. This understated but sophisticated wall lamp has a drum shade made from closely woven raffia in a neutral tone that warms the light to a mellow gold.**

above left **Floodlights—normally associated with outdoor lighting—can be used indoors to fill the space with brilliant light, casting shadows that accentuate the contours of the architecture. These Optec tungsten halogen floodlights by Erco have barn-door covers that can be adjusted to alter** the breadth and direction of the beam. Placed high on the rear wall of a large glass garden room, they add drama after dark.

above center **Considered lighting design gives emphasis to the solid forms in this kitchen-dining room designed by architect Graham Phillips. Blue fluorescent tubes are concealed above the kitchen cabinets and beneath the counter to wash the ceiling with blue light and make the counter appear to float in space. Tiny halogen spotlights recessed above the kitchen counter drench the surface in clean bright light for cooking, and more recessed spotlights in the ceiling of the dining area form pools of light along the tabletop.**

top right **A series of lights recessed into the wall along a landing indicate direction and provide low-level illumination at night, as well as reassurance for guests who may be unfamiliar with the layout of the house. These SKK "Walk on me" spotlights, also suitable for outdoors, are waterproof and come in a choice of colors.**

above right **Lights set at baseboard level on a staircase sharpen the contrast between light and shade, making the distinction between treads and risers more defined. These Monsoon low-glare uplights and step lights by John Cullen Lighting fit flush to the surface and may be used on a horizontal or vertical plane.**

above left **Unlike the original tungsten strip lights,**
which had a cap at each end to house the electrical
connection, modern ones have the connection at the
back and can be set end to end to give a continuous
linear light with no obvious seams. The Philinea
light from the Philips Professional range comes in
lengths of 20 and 40 inches (500 mm and 1 metre).

center left **Wall lights look good in pairs. Emphasized**
by duplication, they also bestow importance on the
object placed between them. The lamps in this hall
are copies of original American Arts and Crafts
designs and flank a table in the same style.

below left **Designed in the 1950s, the sculptural**
Tripod lamp by Serge Mouille still looks modern.
Using the wall as a diffuser, it washes the surface
with light to illuminate the room without glare.

above center **Changes to the layout of this house**
involved the removal of a door at the turn of the
stair, leaving a bare landing. To create interest,
a panel was installed here. It appears to float
unsupported by virtue of concealed lighting that
visually distances the panel from the wall behind.

above right **Unlike ceiling lamps, which often go**
unnoticed when they are switched off, wall lamps
are very visible decorative objects. This distinctive
example was handmade by American craftsman
Sam Mossaedi for an Arts and Crafts house.

center right **Fluorescent strip lighting concealed in a**
light box behind the mirror directs light downward
to highlight the washbasin and enhance the color
and texture of the marble.

below right and opposite **Stairs leading down to**
a basement are lit for safety and effect by square
spotlights recessed low in the wall so the light skims
the treads, accentuating the texture of their carpeted
surface. Similar spotlights are the Square Skirting
Lamps from SKK. Unusually for a basement, the half-
landing through the square archway has a rooflight,
bringing daylight into this naturally dark space.

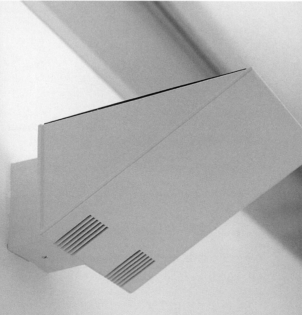

uplighters & downlighters

Uplighters bounce light off the ceiling, which acts as a giant reflector bathing the room in even, diffused light. By contrast, downlighters beam down into the room, flooding the space with bright, direct light.

As sources of ambient light, uplighting and downlighting are usually provided by a number of fixtures spaced so their beams overlap one another to give even illumination. Uplighters may be freestanding floor lights or directional wall-mounted fixtures. Downlighters are usually recessed into the ceiling and are therefore extremely discreet, but because they shed a vertical beam, have a tendency to leave the walls unlit. This can be overcome by choosing directional fixtures that cast light across the surface of the wall.

opposite, above left **An industrial look is achieved by mounting an aluminum spotlight to bare brickwork and running the surface wiring through a metal conduit. The lamp, a Hemisphere spotlight by Box Products, is adjustable, but here it is angled to cast its wide beam downward.**

opposite, main picture and center left **Indirect light reflected off the walls or ceiling gives even, glare-free illumination. These aluminum halogen Lingotto lamps, designed by architect Renzo Piano and made by iGuzzini, can be adjusted horizontally and vertically to direct the beam precisely.**

opposite, below left **Used here as an uplighter, the Tolomeo Faretto wall lamp has an adjustable head with a wide beam. Designed by Michele De Lucchi and Giancarlo Fassina for Artemide, it is made from polished and anodized aluminum.**

opposite, below center **The wedge-shaped Trion uplighter by Erco, mounted high on the wall, directs its beam onto the ceiling to give clean, all-over reflected light.**

opposite, below right **A combination of uplighting and downlighting exaggerates changes in ceiling height along a hall. The uplighter at the end of the passageway seems to beckon you on to a brighter, loftier, more open space.**

this page, above **Downlighters recessed into the ceiling are angled to form arcs of light on a raspberry-pink wall, while wall-mounted uplighters add contrast between foreground and background.**

this page, below left **The uplighter over this writing table is a terracotta cone held in a wall-mounted wrought-iron hoop designed by Garouste and Bonetti from David Gill. Because the light is directed toward the ceiling, task lighting is necessary on the desktop.**

this page, below right **A linear halogen bulb set in a fold of metal with a glass lens completing the third side of the triangle forms the sharp Nelson uplighter. It is supplied as a wall-mounted fixture or freestanding lamp by SKK.**

tracks & spotlights

Spotlights are the ultimate directional lighting and can be adjusted to highlight objects, pictures, architectural features, surfaces, and other areas you wish to accent. Not too distantly related to stage lighting, they produce theatrical effects and add drama to a room. Tracks give spotlights even more flexibility, allowing the light source to be moved anywhere along their length.

Spotlights, by definition, produce a narrow beam of concentrated light, and are horizontally and vertically adjustable, allowing them to be targeted accurately. Mains-voltage spotlights are usually equipped with an incandescent reflector lamp, the interior surface of which is silvered except for the top, thus restricting the angle of beam to no more than 30 degrees. Low-voltage spotlights are installed with a halogen dichroic reflector that is mirrored and faceted to direct light forward and heat backward, giving a bright, cool light.

The range of spotlight fixtures available is extremely varied and includes surface-mounted lights for permanent schemes, floor-standing and clip-on fixtures that offer complete flexibility, and track-mounted designs that give flexibility within a stationary system. Styles vary, too, from simple fixtures that are little more than bulb holders to sleek designs in polished or color-coated metal and etched glass, and stylish architectural lights. The latter are often the work of highly regarded designers and architects, and offer top performance and a pared-down industrial style.

Track lighting design has benefited enormously from the development of low-voltage lighting for domestic interiors. Less obtrusive and more versatile than before, it can be mounted on virtually any horizontal or vertical surface, suspended from cables or rods, or, in the form of a "barewire" system consisting of unsheathed low-voltage cables, strung under tension across a room. Some tracks will carry a number of different but compatible fixtures, allowing pendants, spotlights, and in the case of suspended tracks, uplighters to share the same power source.

far left **Rather than advertise its industrial origins, this spotlight's enclosed lamp and white finish give it a more domestic look.**
left **A modern alternative to the brass picture light, this low-voltage Electro Track system allows lights to be positioned anywhere along the brushed stainless-steel track and adjusted to light the pictures perfectly.**
opposite, above left and above center **Sleek and discreet, track lighting can have decorative value in its own right. This system by Optelma has a pair of slim, silvery tramlines that can be fitted to follow a straight line or smooth curves. Different types of lamp—in this case pendant and spot—can be attached anywhere along its length to give a varied lighting scheme.**
opposite, above right **The Gary fitting by SKK is a neat, fixed spotlight consisting simply of a wall bracket and lamp holder for a low-voltage dichroic bulb. A straight handle, seen here to the left of the fitting, can be used to adjust the direction of the beam.**
opposite, center left **Small and unobtrusive pendant fittings, with translucent shades shielding halogen lamps, hang like tiny globes of white light.**
opposite, below left **This cast-aluminium Pollux halogen spotlight by Erco has an open modular system which, by the addition of colored or contoured filters projecting abstract images such as rippling water or broken glass, offers opportunities to play with lighting effects.**
opposite, below right **In this formal living room with a strictly monochromatic scheme, spotlights fitted to a track that travels the perimeter of the room are angled to emphasize the shape and texture of furnishings.**

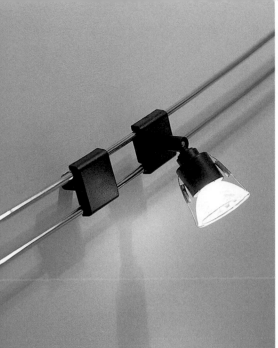

top left **A modern flourish against a traditional paneled ceiling, this metal spiral light, L'Escargot by Serge Mouille from David Gill Gallery, is a fine example of 20th-century design.**

top center **Another 20th-century classic, the 1968 Flower Pot lamp by Verner Panton has recently been brought back into production by Unique Interieur. Originally designed to hang in the atria or stairwells of large buildings in clusters of twenty and more, this hemispherical lamp has always been used individually in domestic interiors.**

top right **This fine Arts and Crafts lantern is carefully proportioned to fit** a lofty, narrow stairwell. The height of the space is celebrated by the design of the metal lantern, whose tall glass panels reflect the shape of the wall panels, and by the prominent ceiling molding that draws the eye up.

above left **Another original Arts and Crafts lamp, custommade to suit the space it occupies, this metal-and-glass chandelier built by the Mica Lamp Co. throws light up to illuminate the beamed ceiling.**

above center **This Holophane prismatic glass lamp with chromed brass hardware is a 1930s original that sheds a bright glare-free light. Hector** Finch sells both original lamps and its own Prism reproduction version.

above right **This classic lamp, the Poulsen PH2/1, designed by Poul Henningsen, has a wide-angled shade to give a broad beam of light. Here, it is attached to a custommade double-angled bracket to allow the position and height to be adjusted.**

opposite, left above and below **Designer David Mullman believes the central light fixture in a room should be luminous and supported by additional light sources to illuminate walls and corners. In this living room the central light is the Archetype pendant by** Boyd Lighting, which has a white fabric shade and satin-nickel stem and canopy. The table in the adjoining dining room is lit by a pair of Reflexion lamps made by Taller Uno. These have a dramatic stepped profile of concentric white cotton cylinders. Each fixture contains one 100-watt bulb and three 60-watt bulbs and is controlled by a dimmer switch.

opposite, right **Inexpensive aluminum IKEA lamps have a functional style that suits them perfectly for an informal dining area where, hung as a pair, they have more visual impact and give a wider spread of light.**

hanging lamps

Hanging lights are generally frowned upon by lighting designers, yet few homes are without them. Roundly condemned for giving an unsubtle, all-over light, they are too often left to provide the only illumination in a room. They can, however, be both functional and decorative within a more complex lighting scheme.

The elaborate plasterwork ceiling center of a period home loses all relevance unless a suitable light fixture is suspended from it, and the chandelier, that mainstay of traditional decoration, has been newly discovered by designers of modern romantic interiors. Likewise, the interest in retro and Scandinavian modern styles has focused attention on the classic lamps of the 20th century, many of which were hanging fixtures. Of course, the center of the ceiling is not the only position for hanging lights, and they need not be hung singly. Indeed, they gain from repetition. Hung in pairs over a dining table or in an evenly spaced series along a hall, they can be as effective as, and have more visual impact than, any downlighter.

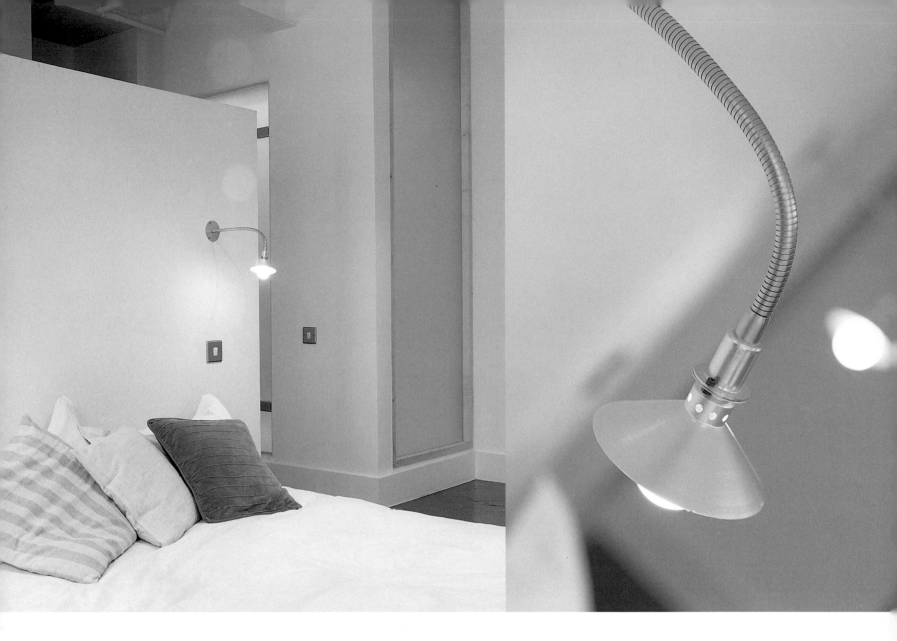

task lighting

The lamps we use when we need extra light to work by are known as task lights. Essential for jobs that involve close concentration and attention to detail, they provide a pool of bright but glare-free light and are precisely adjustable to direct light exactly where it is needed.

The term task lighting immediately brings to mind an image of a desk lamp angled over the page, and the lamp that forged that image is the gooseneck. This classic, designed by Anglepoise in the 1930s and still available today, stands on a heavily weighted base and swivels, pivots, rotates, and tilts with ease and accuracy into stable positions. If the gooseneck seems to be the definitive task lamp, it has not prevented some of the 20th century's great design minds from attempting to improve on it. Many of the new lamps are less bulky and accept halogen tungsten bulbs—plus points that mean they occupy less space on the desktop and give a cleaner, whiter light.

There are, however, other tasks requiring good light for which an angled desk light is not always the most suitable fixture. In a kitchen, for example, where the cook may be working in his or her own shadow, well-focused illumination over the countertop and stove will light up the working area and improve safety. Good lighting is essential for reading, and in the living room a floor lamp or table lamp set at the right height will provide it. In the bedroom, the best reading lights are adjustable, so here, wall-mounted pivoting or flexible gooseneck fixtures, or their tabletop equivalents, will offer the right amount of movement.

opposite **If your taste leans to modern functionalism, the wall-mounted Nelson Flexi by SKK is the perfect bedside lamp. Small and unobtrusive, it has a fully directional flexible stem. The satin-chrome shade is wide angled to give an even spread of light, but opaque so the beam can be directed away from a sleeping partner.** below left **Designed in the early 1970s by Richard Sapper for Artemide and still in production, the iconic Tizio lamp has the distinction of being the first widely available halogen** tungsten light for the home. Conceived as a desk light, but equally at home in the living room, a tall base is available to convert it into a floor-standing reading lamp. below center **Another product of the fertile early 1970s, the 265 designed by Paolo Rizzatto for Arteluce is an extraordinary, elegant fixture, part task light, part wall lamp. Mounted on a swiveling wall bracket, the arm— over 6 feet in length—is balanced for vertical adjustment, and the head is directional. Here, the brackets are** mounted on the walls of a dining room, and the lamps angled to reach over the table. below right **Unlike most kitchen counter lighting, concealed behind a baffle, the Homalux light by Homeier is designed to be seen. The translucent lens sheds a bright, diffused light, and the chrome frame matches other metal kitchen accessories.** bottom left **Frank Lloyd Wright created this reading lamp as an integral part of a wide-armed sofa. A freestanding reproduction of this design is made** by the Yamagiwa USA Corp and is available from Strictly Mission. bottom center **Proof that good design is timeless, the Bestlite by Robert Dudley Best has been in continuous production since it was designed in the 1930s. The wall-mounted version is seen here as a bedside lamp, but desk and floor-standing versions are still made by Best and Lloyd.** bottom right **A basic but efficient design, this aluminum light has an extendable arm and an adjustable head to focus on the work in hand.**

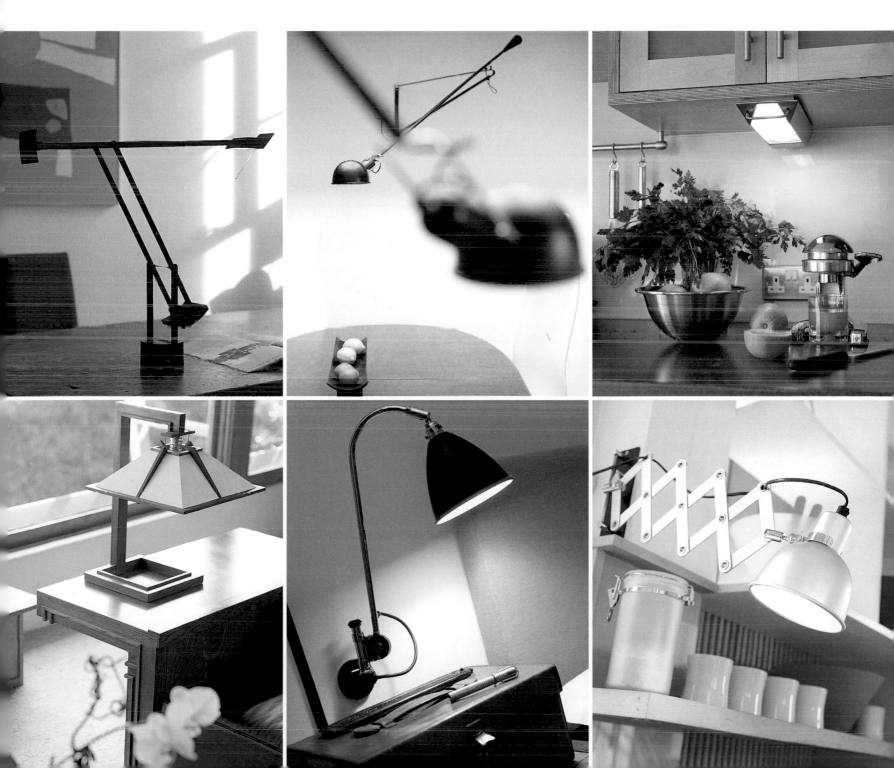

freestanding lamps

Table lamps and floor lamps create an inviting atmosphere by lowering the visual focus to a more intimate level and drawing groups of furniture together in their circle of light.

Movable lamps are usually an addition to a lighting scheme rather than its main feature, and set against a background of ambient or general light they create an expressive balance of light and shade that is somewhat lacking in rooms lit entirely from above.

Table lamps are the most widely used freestanding fixtures and come in all shapes, sizes, and styles. The material the shade is made from has most bearing on the type and color of light it provides. Translucent materials like textiles and parchment give a diffuse light, while shades made from opaque materials such as metal direct light up and down. Closely related to the table lamp is the floor lamp. This umbrella term encompasses everything from a traditional pole lamp down to low level lights that are really oversized table lamps providing functional or decorative light.

above far left and center **The Akari light sculptures created by Japanese artist Isamu Noguchi and produced throughout the second half of the 20th century have become icons of 1950s design. Like all Noguchi lights, the UFI-C (left) and the 22N (center) lamps are Modernist in form but made in the traditional Japanese style from mulberry-bark paper with bamboo ribbing on a metal frame. These lamps are available from the Isamu Noguchi Garden Museum Store.**
above near left **Designed like a contemporary candlestick, the slender Whizz table lamp, by Markus Hürsch for Lumess, has a cylindrical opaque white "candle" that glows with inner light.**
below far left **An unusual light like this rock-shaped floor lamp is more an illuminated object than a light source. By**
highlighting its own slightly granular surface, it draws attention to the contrasting textures of the glass, wicker, limestone, and wood surrounding it. A similar floor lamp is the Glo-ball by Jasper Morrison for Flos.
below center **A period light fixture can be the signature of a historically inspired room scheme or, if the design is distinctive enough, stand alone as a decorative object in a room that does not share its stylistic origins. This antique desk lamp spotlights the silver box standing next to it, amplifying the Art Deco style of both objects.**
below near left **With the light switched on, the Rabane shade from The Conran Shop is transformed from wholesome, natural wickerwork to a glowing mesh weaving shadows across the wall.**

131

above near right **The natural color and grain of wood veneer change dramatically when it is backlit. This woven veneer shade by Peter Wylly is no longer available, but similar contemporary, nonwoven wood designs can be found.**

above center **An uplighter-wallwasher with an industrial aesthetic, this unconventional lamp constructed from recycled materials was designed and made by François Muracciole. More sculptural than decorative, it demands to stand alone where it can be appreciated for its appearance and its lighting effect.**

far right, above and below **This wooden floor-standing lamp was designed by Frank Lloyd Wright for his Arizona home, Taliesin West. Its linear design echoes the vertical rails in the neighboring chair, also designed by Wright. The lamp incorporates a shelf positioned midway below the light to hold a small vase of flowers.**

below near right **More Art Nouveau than Arts and Crafts, this sinuous lily-pad lamp with glass trumpet shades is seen here in the bedroom of a house designed by American Arts and Crafts architects Greene & Greene, where it lends a touch of frivolity. Lamps like this can be found in specialized antique stores and some excellent reproductions are available, such as that from 4 Desk Table Lamps & Shades and Christopher Wray.**

below center left **There is something solidly workmanlike in this table lamp with its five-sided thick wooden base and wide-leaded glass shade. A reproduction of an Arts and Crafts original, it is not seen in its full glory until the lamp is switched on and the colors of the stained glass glow with a jewellike brilliance.**

below center **Designed in the 1960s and currently undergoing a revival, the lava lamp is colorful and fascinating to watch. The clear lamp contains colored water and wax in a contrasting color which, when melted by the heat of the bulb, rises through the water. This Telstar model is now discontinued but Mathmos makes five similar lamps.**

below center right **Elegant and contemporary, with a slightly animated posture, the Kow Tow table lamp by Charlotte Packe has a cream parchment shade and a flexible stem made from disks of anodized, spun aluminum.**

controls

Flexible controls are key to the success of a lighting scheme and should be considered at an early stage in its design. Where they go, what they do, and how they look all have a dramatic effect on the room.

Switches control lighting by turning fixtures on and off, individually or in groups, or by dimming them. Some sophisticated controls can memorize preprogrammed lighting "scenes," allowing you literally to turn on the atmosphere at the flick of a switch. Others can be time- or remote-controlled for convenience.

There is a style of light switch to suit every room, with brass or Bakelite dome switches for period homes and for classic or contemporary interiors, square or rectangular switchplates in black, white, colored, or clear plastic, wood, and virtually any metallic finish you choose. The working part of the control can be a dolly or rocker switch to turn the light on and off, or a knob to operate a dimmer.

opposite and above left **Electrical wiring is usually chased into plasterwork to do its job unseen, but here it is carried over the surface of the wall through a metal conduit to supply a stainless-steel surface-mounted switch. The aesthetic success of surface wiring depends on meticulous installation with straight conduits and neat seams.**

top left **It is unusual to find a bank of four dimmer switches on a single plate, but they can be made to order by specialized electrical suppliers.**

top center **The Meljac push-button momentary dimmer from SKK is a minimal and intelligent control. You flick the button to turn the lights on or off, or press and hold to lower the light to the required level. The switch will store the previous dimmer setting in its memory.**

top right **Virtually invisible with only the control knobs apparent, a clear switchplate gives a sophisticated and discrete finish to a room. Similar clear plastic switchplates are available from Forbes & Lomax.**

above center **When there are a number of lights in the same room, controls can be arranged in rows on a single switchplate, or as here, arranged singly and in pairs on separate plates. Old-fashioned dolly switches are suitable for a traditionally furnished room and look best on a plain, flat plate.**

above right **Designer Patti Seidman believes that you turn lights on and off more often than you adjust the level of light and finds that the Lutron Diva switch, which has a large on-off rocker switch and a separate lever to dim the light, conforms to those priorities.**

KITCHENS

AS THE BARRIERS BETWEEN LIVING ROOMS AND KITCHENS COME DOWN, THE PLACE WHERE

WE COOK BECOMES OPEN TO SCRUTINY—ALL THE MORE REASON TO REASSESS THE WAY

IT LOOKS AND WORKS. CABINETS AND SURFACES COME IN EVERY KIND OF WOOD, STONE,

LAMINATED AND PAINTED FINISHES, OR IN SUPER-CHIC MATERIALS LIKE GLASS AND METAL.

AND FAUCETS, SINKS, AND APPLIANCES ARE MORE STYLISH AND EFFICIENT THAN EVER.

kitchen units

A new openness in living space has brought changes into the kitchen. No longer hidden behind closed doors, it is a place to be shared with family and friends—and it must look good.

Over the last few decades, the kitchen has undergone a remarkable shift in status. From a utilitarian space for the preparation of food, it has become an integral part of the home, where cooking, eating, and entertaining take place side by side. Accordingly, it is furnished as thoughtfully, and expensively, as the living room. The idea of a kitchen in which you would eat out of choice rather than necessity emerged in the 1970s, when a pine farmhouse kitchen with a scrubbed table was the ideal. The image was one of warmth and hospitality, the hub of family life. Now, instead of living in the kitchen, open-plan layouts have changed the emphasis so it is more a case of cooking in the living room—a setup made all the more possible by improvements in air extraction and virtually silent appliances.

Kitchen units, too, have moved on, and cabinets faced with metal, glass, and even stone are as much an option as polished or painted wood and laminates. Even the familiar finishes are developing with changing trends, as exotic wood veneers and high-gloss laminates give a sharper, urban look.

left **Appearing to defy the laws of gravity, this cooking alcove suspended from the ceiling allows an uninterrupted sweep of glossy black floor to give a feeling of continuity and space. The alcove was custommade, though some IKEA kitchen carcasses were adapted and used in its construction.**

opposite, above left **Sharp contrast conveys urban sophistication in this slick yellow and black kitchen with Formica-laminated cabinets and slate countertops.**

opposite, above right **This traditionally inspired blue and cream kitchen has an island unit at its center to make practical use of a large floor area.**

opposite, center left **Designed to appear as a heavy stone block hovering above the floor, this unit is cantilevered from the wall with additional support from a ceiling-mounted pillar, which also carries the power supply. The unit is faced with beige pietro laro limestone and has spray-lacquered doors.**

opposite, center **Horizontal lines dominate this kitchen where the stripes of the tall cabinet are echoed in the wooden banding of the wall cabinets.**

opposite, center right **Made from distinctively grained crown-cut oak, this horizontal unit provides efficient storage and is a good-looking piece of furniture.**

opposite, below left **Built from IKEA units fitted with custommade composite-board doors, the angles and curves of these cabinets are linked by their strong colors.**

opposite, below center **In order to screen and contain the clutter of cooking, this rank of cabinets is enclosed on three sides by taller panels, with electrical sockets built into the upstand.**

opposite, below right **Cubic cupboards arranged like building blocks make full use of an impressive wall height.**

Architect-designed kitchens have always had the edge on those from standard lines, but the gap between the two is gradually narrowing as kitchen manufacturers are willing to build cabinets or at least customize existing designs to meet individual demands. This break from strictly modular design has opened the way for more interesting and inventive use of space.

Conventional built-in kitchens take the form of deep floor-standing base units with smaller wall-mounted cabinets above, but in the interests of creating a more open, spacious effect, wall units are now used more sparingly. Where they are used, ease of access has been addressed with tambour shutters and up-and-over doors offering space-saving alternatives to side-hinged doors that swing out at head height. If wall cabinets are lost, storage must be found elsewhere, and one of the most efficient alternatives is to build a bank of floor-to-ceiling closets with shelves, drawers, and racks, and incorporating the refrigerator and freezer. In most kitchens, a wall like this would supply enough storage to allow countertops—often seconded as overflow shelf space—to be left clear.

New ideas for base units also contribute to a more spacious look, with some designers exploring the possibilities of "floating" units. These are cabinets supported on strong, cantilevered brackets from an adjoining wall or suspended from joists in the ceiling. The result is an unbroken sweep of floor and an impression of space and continuity. Where it is not possible to physically lift the units off the floor, a similar effect can be achieved by recessing the kickboard at the foot of the cabinets and installing lights invisibly in the space.

opposite, left **This kitchen was reinvented using some carcasses salvaged from the existing cupboards. The new composite doors were professionally spray-painted for a perfect finish, in colors inspired by an exhibition catalog for London's Design Museum. Laminate counters and polished aluminium handles enhance the retro style.**
opposite, above right **Two solutions to the problem of small-scale storage: a rack of glass jars holds seasonings where they are easy to identify, and neat square drawers with finger-hole pulls are just the right size for dry ingredients, small utensils, string, scissors, and other vital but hard-to-place items.**
opposite, center right **Shimmering aluminum-framed sandblasted-glass cabinets, steel appliances, and white marble counters create a cool translucent**

effect. **Wide drawers and concealed storage mean that nothing needs to be left on the surfaces to detract from the pale perfection of the materials.**
opposite, below right **Pan scrubbers, brushes, and cloths are an inescapable part of the kitchen-sink landscape, but this tilt-out sponge tray by Feeny, available in stainless steel or plastic, fits into the fascia in front of the sink to hide them from view.**
this page, top left **A modern interpretation of a pantry, this cabinet opens to give a clear view of its entire contents. Storage is divided between open shelves and metal racks on the insides of the doors; both are adjustable so they can be moved to suit changing storage demands. The interior of the pantry is made from pale birch plywood, which reflects light into the shelf cavities.**

this page, above left **Concentrating storage in a wall of floor-to-ceiling cabinets makes economical use of space and results in a "hidden kitchen" where all food and utensils are concealed, leaving counters clear. Here, storage is arranged in three tiers. The middle cabinets, housing small appliances such as a coffeemaker and toaster, have flip-down doors that can be used as surfaces when using those items.**
this page, above right **A combination of sleek materials adds glamour to this conventional galley kitchen. The base cabinets are veneered with dark-stained Italian poplar in contrast to the light maple and sandblasted glass wall units. The work surface and square sink are made from the same silky black honed granite. The sink is set on an open shelf with half-height cabinets beneath.**

surfaces

Your kitchen countertop and sink protection must be up to the job: choose high-performance materials that offer good looks, too.

The ideal work surface is durable, hygienic, quiet, stain resistant, and heatproof; but as no one material can claim ownership to all of these qualities, a compromise must be reached, and appearance is invariably the deciding factor. The choice lies between natural materials like wood and stone, which tend to complement each other, or synthetics such as laminates and resins, which, depending on their style and quality, can be successfully combined with cabinets made of natural or manmade materials.

opposite, above **This brilliant blue-veined counter and sink-back are made from a Brazilian granite, azul macauba, which contains precious lapis lazuli.**

opposite, center left **Damage from sharp knives and hot pans can be removed from natural wood surfaces by rubbing them with abrasive paper. Oil newly sanded surfaces to seal and protect them.**

opposite, center **This chef's trolley is topped with a functional beech-wood chopping board and slides neatly away into a cabinet when not in use.**

opposite, center right **This breakfast bar is built from custommade laminated board in a barcode stripe designed by Filer & Cox.**

opposite, below left **An unusual large-scale terrazzo, this crazy patchwork of marble fragments is ground smooth to produce a practical but eccentric surface.**

opposite, below center **Using the same batique blue limestone for the floor and work surfaces gives a sense of space and consistency. The soft gray-blue of the stone has an affinity with the light elm cabinets.**

opposite, below right **This wavy-edged counter is formed from thick plywood cut to shape, sanded, and sealed so the layers of laminated wood show as striped edging.**

above right **The concrete counter and side panel, cast on site by a local contractor, form a continuous hard shell around the stained and pickled white ash veneer cabinets.**

right **Smooth, cool, and famously ideal for pastry making, marble is also vulnerable to staining if not properly sealed and cared for. This 1½-inch- (4-cm-) thick Carrara marble has a silky honed finish—less hard- and new-looking than polished marble. Large slabs mean joints are kept to a minimum.**

this page, above left and top right **Sleek and cool, glass is a sophisticated and surprisingly practical choice of countertop for a modern kitchen. This kitchen, by VX Design, is part of an open-plan living area and uses translucent materials for most of its hard surfaces. The island is wrapped in toughened etched glass, as is the narrow arching bar.**

this page, above right **This shelf in a cook's kitchen is often filled to overflowing, but a low rail around the edge prevents bottles from slipping off the smooth surface.**

opposite, above left **Stainless steel for the counter and high sink-back offers a neutral yet lively balance for the vivid pink units in this family kitchen. Most stainless-steel counters are made to measure and can be supplied with integral sinks in** a variety of configurations. The splash protector, too, has been customized to incorporate a narrow shelf along its entire length to hold frequently used dishes, glasses, and ingredients.

opposite, above right **Instead of imposing its own style, a stainless-steel counter takes on the character of its surroundings. The cabinets in this dazzling white kitchen are made from a high-gloss laminate in the Op-art Morphscape pattern designed by its owner, Karim Rasheed. The stainless-steel counter and sink-back reflect the predominantly white laminate and appear light, bright, and silvery.**

opposite, center left **The great advantage of stainless steel is that it can be formed into many shapes, so different components can be made from the same material to give complete continuity. Straight rods** along the front of the work surface are handy for hanging dishtowels or utensils while you work.

opposite, below left **Brushed steel is the most forgiving metal surface, its soft sheen tactfully camouflaging fingermarks. Designed and made by John Barman, Inc., this kitchen shows off the quality of the metal and its industrial aesthetic by keeping detail to a minimum with perfectly flat door and drawer fronts punctuated by tiny functional knobs.**

opposite, below right **The epitome of a professional-style kitchen, stainless steel is used over all the main surfaces here, including the island countertop. Tough, hygienic, and heatproof, it can stand up to the rigors of a hard-working kitchen. The only drawback is that it can be noisy to work on, but this can be overcome with proper insulation.**

plumbing

Good plumbing is an essential aspect of kitchen design and one that has not been neglected by architects and designers, who offer faucets and sinks that are both striking in appearance and supremely efficient.

No kitchen can function without a ready, reliable, and easily controlled water supply and a sink in which to rinse food, wash hands, and do the dishes. Plumbing may have a less than glamorous image, but it is an area of interest for designers, intrigued by the engineering and aesthetic challenge. Distinguished designers like Arne Jacobsen and Philippe Starck have designed faucets that achieved iconic status, but there are many more, conceived by unsung designers, that fulfill their purpose with style and efficiency.

Kitchen faucets are made to a number of basic patterns, the oldest being the bibcock—a deck- or wall-mounted faucet with a spout and crosshead handle. Mixers deliver hot and cold water from the same spout, but may have separate handwheels or levers to control the supply. They can be deck or wall mounted, traditional or modern in style, and are put in via two or three holes drilled in the surface.

top row, far left **Designed to appear smaller than it really is, this unusual portrait-shaped stainless-steel sink is recessed into the wall as well as the counter. The wall-mounted Vola mixer with swivel spout was designed by Arne Jacobsen.**

top row, center left **Bib faucets on upstands match the traditional style of a ceramic sink and are set high enough to avoid catching dishes when they are lifted in and out of the sink.**

top row, center right **A double-bowl sink is useful for food preparation, but provision must be made for draining. Many manufacturers supply drainer baskets or trays to fit their sinks as separate accessories. A swivel-spout mixer like this elegantly arched monobloc faucet is essential for a double-bowl sink. A similar tap is the Petita by Grohe.**

top row, near left **In a kitchen where superfluous detail is kept to a minimum and low-sheen surfaces prevail, the satin-steel Arwa-Twin, with a pull-out spout, by Gemini Bath and Kitchen Products fills the stainless-steel double sink mounted under a thick marble surface.**

middle row, far left **A wall-mounted hospital faucet transplants smoothly into a small kitchen where its slender shape and pivoting spout fit the restricted space. Similar hospital- and laboratory-style mixers are available from T & S Brass.**

middle row, center left **An inventive plumber has created this faucet from pipes and valves usually hidden from view. Check local building and water regulations before constructing your own version.**

middle row, center right **As neat and compact as the circular sink it fills, this monobloc faucet has a single lever that controls both temperature and flow. The Allegra range by Hansgrohe has similar designs with and without a pull-out spray.**

middle row, near left **A nostalgic style for a country kitchen, this mixer, similar to the Colonial by Bristan and the Victorian models by Harrington Brass and Gemini, has a brushed finish for a lime-worn effect.**

bottom row, far left **Faucets with a pull-out brush do not comply with regulations in some countries, but the alternative pull-out spray is more widely accepted. The Europlus by Grohe is similar in appearance to the one shown here, but has a spray for rinsing vegetables and sluicing plates.**

bottom row, center left **White ceramic levers give an arched monobloc tap a period look.**

bottom row, center right **A compact swan-neck monobloc similar to the Ostende by Herbeau supplies a small hammered metal sink used for preparing vegetables.**

bottom row, near left **Plumbing goes back to basics in this rustic kitchen with a ceramic sink mounted on a countertop and supplied by garden taps on the wall above.**

Monobloc fixtures are the newest type and are consequently modern in design. Deck mounted through a single hole in the sink or work surface, they consist of a spout with separate handles to control the hot and cold flow or a single lever handle that controls temperature and flow at once. The latest developments in faucet design are mixer versions with a third handle that allows purified drinking water as well as hot and cold water to flow from the same spout, and monoblocs that incorporate a pull-out hose and rinsing spray. Finishes are many and varied, ranging from shiny, satin, and antique metals to colored plain and speckled effects.

The kitchen sink, once a symbol of drudgery, has shaken off its depressing associations and is now a visually important feature of

the kitchen. Sinks may be made from ceramic, stainless steel, brass, synthetic or real stone, and even wood, and are set into, under, or between work surfaces. Various configurations are available, of which a single sink and drainer unit is the most basic, and an angled sink to fit the corner of a kitchen probably the most unusual. Double sinks are a popular choice, and many can be equipped with a waste-disposal unit to deal with wet waste from food preparation. Sinks must incorporate some provision for draining in the form of an attached draining board, grooves cut into the adjoining waterproof work surface, or a basket that fits into one of the sinks. The major exception is where an additional sink is inset into an island unit for the purpose of straining food from saucepans.

opposite, top left **This traditional bridge mixer with an upwardly angled "cranked" spout was chosen in preference to the arching swan-neck type for its compact shape. Made by Samuel Heath, the shiny chrome finish adds a sparkle to the predominantly white scheme.**

opposite, above left **A modified shower mixer makes an interesting kitchen faucet with a flexible spout, but may not comply with regulations governing water equipment in all areas. A similar effect can be achieved with a purpose-made faucet designed for** commercial kitchens, such as the Pro-chef by Brass & Traditional Sinks.

opposite, right **A classic minimalist design by architect and designer Dieter Sieger, the Tara Classic mixer faucet and soap dispenser produced by Dornbracht make a fitting centerpiece for this practical stainless-steel sink area. Note the downlighters installed flush into the underside of the wall cabinets to illuminate the sink and work surface.**

this page, main picture **In this sleek, rather masculine kitchen, the overall effect is one of understated luxury.**

The work surface with its integral sink is made from black honed granite, which has a gleaming satin surface far removed from the hard gloss of polished stone. The splash protector is a continuous stainless-steel surface, brushed to a low sheen. The faucet, a design icon, is the Vola KV1 kitchen mixer by Arne Jacobsen.

top right **All-metal mixers with lever handles have a minimalist, almost clinical appearance, but the clean and functional design that makes them so suitable for use in hospitals and laboratories is equally appropriate in** the kitchen. This faucet is made by T & S Brass, and similar designs can be found in lines made for hospitals by other manufacturers, such as Barber Wilsons.

above right **Another architects' favorite, little known on the commercial scene, this faucet with star-shaped handles—made in Denmark by Toni Armatur—is a beautifully pared-down design, engineered to last. Teamed, as it is here, with an integral stainless-steel sink and countertop, it contributes toward the air of professional efficiency in the kitchen.**

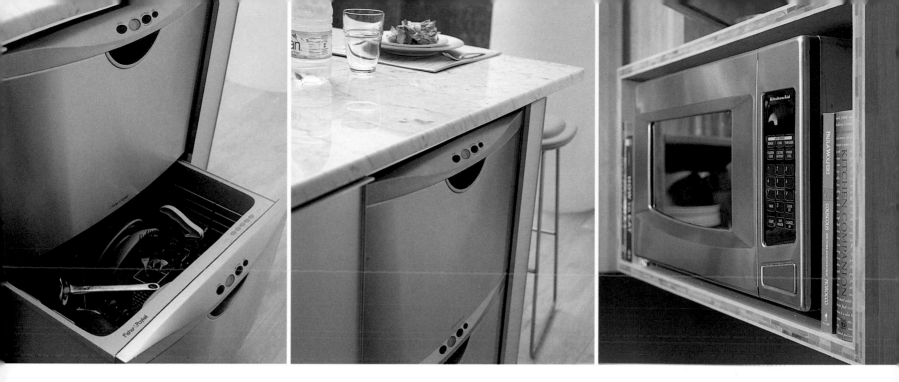

appliances

Not so long ago kitchen appliances were hidden away, only evident when they shuddered into action. Now, technology has reordered priorities, and like Victorian children, they are seen but rarely heard.

Appliances are the essential working parts of a kitchen and exert a strong influence on its style. Freestanding models are weighty and solid, with a distinctive character. In recent years, stoves and fridges have increased in size, with industrial models entering the domestic environment and farmhouse stoves moving to the city. Built-in appliances are sleek, streamlined, and make economical use of space in urban kitchens, where the coffeemaker is now as likely to be built in as the oven or dishwasher. Designed for looks as well as performance, these machines are no longer hidden behind cabinet doors and décor panels, but have become fashion items, carrying the household equivalent of designer labels. In tandem with aesthetic developments, technology has improved household machines with efficient and quiet running, while energy labeling means consumers can choose those that make least impact on the environment and their pockets.

opposite, above **A monolithic double-door refrigerator like this one from the professional Monogram range by General Electric could dominate a kitchen, but its stainless-steel finish offers some camouflage amid the other metallic surfaces. Inside, the space is divided into temperature zones to provide prime storage conditions for different foods.**
opposite, below left **A stainless-steel dishwasher from the Gallery line by Frigidaire is quiet-running and fits the industrial aesthetic of this all-metal**

kitchen. Part of its attraction is its simple design with discreet controls and an easy-to-grip handle.**
opposite, below center **This Monogram microwave by General Electric is actually a countertop model, but it has been slotted into purpose-made housing at eye level to give a fully built-in look and to leave the work surfaces clear.**
opposite, below right **Framed in an alcove, this bright blue fridge-freezer by Boffi adds a lively splash of color to a neutral kitchen.**

above left and center **An intelligent design, the DishDrawer dishwasher by Fisher & Paykel has two independently operated pull-out washing units. One can be used alone when there are only a few dishes to wash, or they can be used together on different settings to wash delicate crystal and heavily soiled saucepans.**
top right **In a small kitchen where open shelves have been built instead of wall cabinets to provide high-level storage, the KitchenAid microwave is placed in a wall-mounted box shelf,**

slightly deeper than the rest, with just enough space left over to slip in a few favorite cookbooks.**
above right **This fridge-freezer stands at one end of a rank of built-in units, and although it is freestanding, it has clearly been planned into the layout at an early stage. Base and wall cabinets are positioned to leave a space into which it fits perfectly, and its stainless-steel finish implies a relationship with the work surface and other appliances, though they are not all from the same manufacturer.**

this page, above **A built-under oven with a stove-top above it looks like a single cooking unit, but is more streamlined than a freestanding stove and saves space in a small kitchen. Usually the stove and oven are selected from the same line, but appliances from different manufacturers can be teamed up to give the combination of features required. Here, an oven from the Gallery line by Frigidaire is installed under Amana natural-gas burners.**

this page, below left **This curved concrete counter was cast on site with plywood molds to form indentations into which the burner units were later fitted. Modular burners like these by Smeg allow a more flexible kitchen layout, especially when the work surface is not a conventional shape.**

this page, below right **Specially designed for healthy eaters, the extra-wide burner unit on the Viking 36-inch (91-cm) range incorporates a griddle-simmer plate.**

opposite, above left and above center **The migration of the professional stove into the home kitchen is complete, and heavy-duty ranges like this Viking freestanding model have become a familiar feature. Built for efficiency, every detail is designed to make cooking safer and easier. The pan supports, for example, are made from strong cast iron configured to support small pans without tipping and to allow large, heavy pans to slide over them without lifting.**

opposite, above right **Burner covers leave the kitchen looking neat when they are not in use. This Gaggenau stove has a divided shot-blasted aluminum lid that folds down over two or four burners.**

opposite, center left **A powerful hood is essential when the kitchen forms part of an open-plan living area, and this Miele Combiset hood is available as an extractor, venting to the outside, or as a filter, cleaning and recirculating the air.**

opposite, below left **For convenience, store frequently used utensils around the stove. Here, a hanging rod extends across the back, and the Bosch hood has been equipped with an optional chrome wire shelf strong enough to hold saucepans.**

opposite, below right **The Viking range comes in four sizes, from 30–60 inches (75–150 cm) wide. It was designed for use in professional kitchens, but has a standard depth measurement that allows it to slot easily between built-in units.**

opposite, above left **The chimneybreast and alcove were specially built to accommodate this reconditioned 1940s Aga, with a "supporting" beam from a reclamation yard for authenticity. Reproduction Agas in 1930s styles are available for those who want a period look without tracking down an original.**

opposite, above center **Modern Agas, while still distinctively traditional in style, offer a choice of fuels and come in a range of classic and fashionable colors, including the original cream.**

opposite, above right **A combination microwave oven is stacked above a single oven, both from Bosch, creating a mid-height cooking unit at the end of a run of cabinets.**

this page, above left **A pair of ceramic burner units by General Electric, virtually flush with the countertop, sit neatly side by side above a matching wide built-under oven.**

this page, above center **An inset single burner is a useful addition to the main stove in a large kitchen; in addition many manufacturers produce independent built-in wok burners.**

this page, above right **A refined version of the industrial range, this has twin ovens, a wide burner unit, and an integral back and hood. Similar models are made by Smeg and Britannia.**

below far left **Independent burner modules like this Domino unit by Smeg allow you to place a stove-top where you need it.**

below center and near left center **In this sleek kitchen, cooking appliances are centralized in a single stack, with a built-in coffeemaker perched at eye level above the Miele double oven. A tall, pull-out pantry separates the ovens from the nearby Sub-Zero fridge.**

below near left **An island unit composed of an oval stainless-steel countertop with Smeg burners supported on a cylindrical wooden cabinet makes a contemporary statement.**

155

BATHROOMS

WHEN A TUB CAN COST AS MUCH AS A FAMILY CAR, YOU KNOW THE BATHROOM HAS BECOME

A FASHION ITEM. MATERIAL IS THE WATCHWORD: BATHTUBS ARE NOW MADE IN ANYTHING

FROM LOW-COST ACRYLICS TO INDUSTRIAL STAINLESS STEEL AND LUXURY LIMESTONE. BASINS

ARE FASHIONED FROM GLASS, MARBLE, AND WOOD AS WELL AS COOL GLOSSY CERAMICS, AND

WALLS AND FLOORS ARE SURFACED IN FINISHES AS DIVERSE AS CONCRETE, WOOD, AND MOSAIC.

fixtures

Bathroom design is increasingly flexible and is now more likely to be tailored to match the owner's lifestyle than any preconceived formal. Yet the essential fixtures are still a tub, washbasin, and toilet, with a separate shower enclosure and bidet as optional but desirable extras.

In most bathrooms, the bathtub is the dominating feature. Tubs don't have to be bought as part of a set, though some manufacturers offer a small choice of shapes to complement their ceramic fixtures. Bathtubs are most commonly made from acrylic, enameled steel, or porcelain-enameled cast iron, but new materials such as acrylic resin—a warm-to-the-touch nonchip substitute for cast iron—are becoming more popular. Apart from standard materials, bathtubs in stainless steel, limestone, or hardwood are an option, but they are usually made to order and therefore more expensive.

Bathtub shapes vary widely, and in addition to the standard rectangular tub that comes in sizes to fit most bathrooms, there are tapered bathtubs for small spaces, corner tubs for awkward spaces, and freestanding versions in traditional and modern styles. Antique rolltop tubs made from cast iron with ball-and-claw feet can sometimes be bought in original condition from architectural salvage yards or restored from dealers specializing in antique bathroom fixtures. Alternatively, reproduction rolltop bathtubs made from cast iron or acrylic resin are available from most bathroom suppliers. Most modern freestanding tubs are made from acrylic resin and stand alone or enclosed inside a purpose-built cabinet.

A shower is a high priority for most for new bathrooms. Where space is limited, it can be mounted over the tub, but a separate enclosure or area is always the ideal. Those who prefer showering to bathing may opt for a large shower area instead of a but (but realtors maintain that properties with at least one bathtub are easier to sell than those with none). A shower can be bought as a self-contained cabinet or built on site using the existing walls, new partition walls, glass-brick walls, or safety-glass shower panels, with a sliding, folding, hinged, or pivoting glass door. The enclosure must be lined with tiles or some other waterproof surface, and sealed to prevent seepage. A shower tray, generally made from glazed ceramic, enameled steel, or acrylic, can form the floor. Alternatively, in a bathroom

above left **The custommade neon green Plexiglass shower screen and vanity shelf add a lively, reflective dimension in a small shower room.**

center left **The glowing interior of this circular shower enclosure was constructed on site by gluing together three layers of ¼-inch (6-mm) birch plywood. Veneer was applied to conceal the horizontal joint, and the whole surface was sealed against moisture with several coats of marine varnish.**

below left **The walls in this wet room were coated with natural sand and cement render and made waterproof with a clear sealant. On the floor, the honed limestone slabs are spaced to allow water to drain through to an outlet beneath.**

below center **Mosaic tiles in assorted shades of blue bring color into this shower room, and a wall of textured glass bricks allows daylight in.**

below right **This shower enclosure was designed to let natural light spill through. The unit comprises a curve of sandblasted glass custommade to fit**

around a circular stainless-steel base—both were made to order by local contractors.

opposite, above **The airy character of this bathroom has been preserved by zoning the space with custommade transparent glass panels.**

opposite, below left **A circular enclosure formed from frosted glass makes a roomy shower cabinet, top-lit for brilliant illumination. A shower tower, similar to the Taron by Grohe, supplies water through a fixed showerhead and hand spray.**

opposite, below center **The classical style of this bathroom demanded unobtrusive fixtures, and the frameless shower door, similar to those in the Majestic line, allows the eye to pass through to the honey-colored stone-lined interior.**

opposite, below right **In this wet room, oblong glass bricks shield the shower area. The floor is tiled with limestone, and the walls are finished in hardwall plaster. The porous surfaces were all treated with a stone-waterproofing sealant by Lithofin.**

designed as a wet room with walls and floor fully waterproofed, the shower needs no enclosure and the water escapes through a central drain in the floor. Showers perform well only if there is adequate water pressure, but where the pressure is too low, a pump can be installed to boost the flow.

To meet the demand for different shapes, sizes, and styles, washbasins are made in a wide variety of materials, with glazed ceramic basins being the traditional choice. These are available in a range of colors, including the classic white, and are tough, easy to clean, and available to buy off the shelf. With a choice of pedestal, wall-mounted, inset, and under-mounted countertop models, washbasins are often designed as part of a set of matching fixtures, taking some of the decision-making out of the process of bathroom design. However, like baths, interesting stand-alone models are available if you want the basin to be the focus of the room. Beautiful and surprisingly resilient, glass basins can also be bought readymade, but the choice is limited to small or medium round bowls in a limited number of colors and finishes. However, this restriction only applies to readymade basins; custommade glass bowls

opposite, above left **A compact design, ideal for a small half-bath, this tubby wall-mounted basin by Agape goes by the descriptive name of Cheese.**

opposite, above center **This satinized-glass basin is part of an all-in-one wall-mounted unit incorporating a mixer faucet, plumbing, and bracket and known as the Pollux 1. The combination of translucent and reflective materials gives it a lack of solidity that makes it a good choice for a small bathroom.**

opposite, above right **Concrete is favored for its industrial chic and can be used to custom-make hardwearing surfaces of all kinds. This basin, designed and cast by Philip Wish, has a wide, shallow bowl and deep ledges at the sides.**

opposite, below left **Designed to relieve the morning rush hour when everyone is getting ready at the same time, this long glass design is more streamlined than the usual twin basins. Custom made by Jeff Bell, it is shallow and gently angled to provide efficient emptying.**

opposite, center right **Masculine in character, this straight-sided rectangular basin made from 12-inch- (30-mm-) thick gray limestone is built wide enough for more enthusiastic washing than a smaller basin would allow. The mixer spout and pop-up plug are placed on one side, and the handles are installed at the front of the countertop.**

opposite, below right **In a small bathroom where there is little scope for adventurous decoration, fixtures with an unusual design feature make the space more interesting. The wall-mounted Scola basin by Duravit, for example, has a circular bowl set into a rectangular surround.**

above **The shape of this square basin from Colourwash is accentuated by its setting on a custommade brushed stainless-steel base. Inside, the sharp angles give way to smooth curves for easier cleaning.**

right **Stainless-steel fixtures give the bathroom a functional look, but this custommade basin's elegant shape eliminates any hint of institutional severity.**

above **A high-level cast-iron cistern is usually an original fixture, but makers of traditional bathroom fixtures, such as B.C. Sanitan and Vintage Plumbing, supply ceramic ones for a similar look.**

right **In this circular frosted-glass cloakroom pod, the ultra-modern basin and toilet stand in the center of the space with drainage ducted through the floor. Overhead spotlights combine with polished steel and glass to gleaming effect.**

opposite, above left **In small bathrooms, a toilet with a flush operated by a valve instead of a cistern can help save space. They are widespread in the United States, where the water pressure is high enough to provide adequate through-put.**

opposite, center left **In a sophisticated setting, a stainless-steel toilet has a stylish industrial aesthetic. This one is wall mounted on a sturdy bracket with a concealed cistern. Similar stainless-steel models are made by Santric.**

opposite, above right **A narrow rectangular cistern and conical bowl combine in the uncompromisingly contemporary Starck close-coupled toilet by Duravit.**

opposite, below left **A floor-standing bidet with a traditional waisted shape, the London bidet is shown here with a rounded crosshead Leonardo faucet from C.P. Hart.**

opposite, below center **The wall-hung model of the Starck toilet, with a concealed cistern, is the ultimate minimalist design.**

opposite, below right **For a luxury look with a modern edge, choose fixtures with smoothly rounded edges but no extraneous decoration. The Allora by Jacuzzi is similar in shape to this wall-mounted toilet.**

can be produced in much larger sizes and non-standard shapes and designs. At the more exclusive end of the market are basins made from unconventional materials such as wood, stone, marble, plywood, and, less expensively, stainless steel.

Toilets come in styles to suit every taste, but one practical way in which they can differ is in the type of cistern they have. Most common is the close-coupled cistern that sits at the back of the bowl giving the appearance of an all-in-one unit. Low-level cisterns are wall-mounted with a flush pipe connecting the cistern to the bowl, and traditional high-level cisterns are wall-mounted on decorative brackets with a long pipe to the bowl and a pull chain to operate the flush. Concealed cisterns, usually used with back-to-wall and wall-mounted toilets, are installed behind a false wall or panel with only the flush handle or button visible.

Bidets are a convenient way to deal with personal hygiene and are usually situated alongside the toilet. They are filled by a monobloc faucet with an directional nozzle to angle the water flow, and, like toilets, can be floor-standing or wall-mounted.

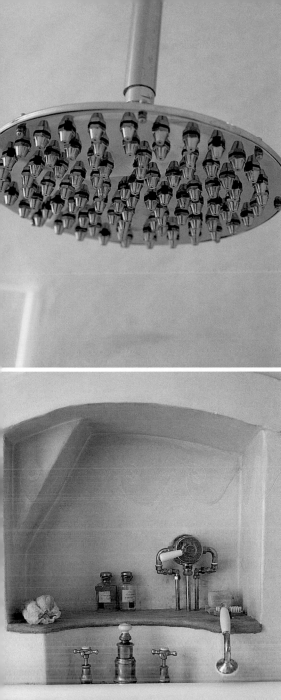

faucets & controls

Adjusting water temperature is a matter of safety as well as convenience, so controls must be easy to operate by everyone, including children and the elderly. Clear labeling is vital, particularly in showers, where a handle turned the wrong way can result in a rush of scalding water.

Bathroom faucets come in three main formats: three-hole mixers where the handles and spout are separate; mixers that are single units incorporating spout and handles or a single lever; and traditional "pillar" faucets with separate outlets for hot and cold. Basin mixers often incorporate a pop-up plug, while bathtub faucets may also feed a shower, with a handle to divert water from one function to the other. Shower controls can be thermostatic or mechanical: thermostatic controls deliver water at a preset temperature, while mechanical showers are adjusted manually to achieve the right temperature.

top row, far left **Overhead showers give a thorough drenching, and in a large enclosure, two sprays provide even coverage. However, two showers deliver twice the volume of water, so a large drain will be needed for efficient emptying. A similar overhead shower is the Aktiva by Hansgrohe.**

top row, center left **These four-square chunky traditional-looking controls are mixers for the bath and shower. The chrome crosshead handles are the Regent design by Barber Wilsons.**

top row, center right **A dual-control thermostatic shower mixer has one handle to control the water flow and another to adjust the temperature. This fixture by Hansgrohe is now available as a design that has both handles on one plate.**

top row, near left **Designed to remain free of mineral deposits, this showerhead has tiny projections that keep the jets clear. A similar showerhead is the Fez by Agape.**

middle row, far left **White enameled faucets were popular in the 1970s and 1980s, and look good in an all-white bathroom. Here, the four crosshead handles are mixer controls for the bath and a showerhead above.**

middle row, center left **This recessed thermostatic shower mixer adjusts the water temperature at the touch of a lever. A similar control from Barber Wilsons with** a round or square plate and china lever comes in unlacquered brass, which will tarnish naturally.

middle row, center right **This minimal shower wand, part of the Vola suite designed more than 40 years ago by Arne Jacobsen, is a modern classic.**

middle row, near left **A set of period brassware complete with shower mixer, faucets and spray is quite a find, but should always be fully refurbished before plumbing in. Similar reproduction sets are available in traditional lines.**

bottom row, far left **The successor to this modern single-control thermostatic mixer from the Axor line by Hansgrohe is the Aktivated thermostatic shower.**

bottom row, center left **A shower spray with a ceramic handle often comes as part of a traditional telephone-style bath-shower mixer set like those in the Antique and Georgian lines by Samuel Heath.**

bottom row, center right **Genuine antique faucets give an air of authenticity to a traditional bathroom. Track down original fixtures through antique-bathroom dealers or at architectural salvage yards.**

bottom row, near left **A relaxing drench or an invigorating massage jet—this setup provides both, with a 12 inch (300 mm) Waterloo shower rose by C.P. Hart and an Aktiva showerhead by Hansgrohe that offers a choice of spray patterns.**

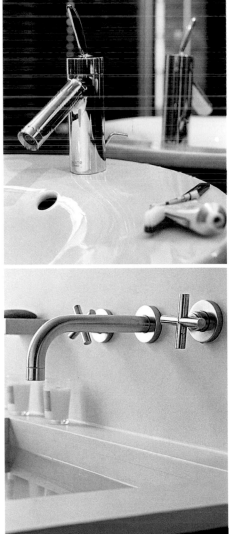

opposite, above left **Designed in the 1960s and still in production today, Arne Jacobsen's Vola tap has inspired a whole generation of plumbing fixtures. It is minimalist in style with no mechanical parts visible, and there are scores of variations available, including shower fixtures, pillar faucets and deck- and wall-mounted mixers like this two-handled chrome version with a fixed spout.**

opposite, above right **The indulgence of a freestanding tub is just as appropriate in a modern bathroom as a traditional one—a fact recognized by designers of brassware, who now produce suitably contemporary fixtures. This beautifully simple floor-mounted faucet is the Vola 090FM. The handles are mounted separately elsewhere.**

opposite, below left **Size and scale should always be taken into consideration when selecting faucets. Here a chunky bridge mixer is more in proportion to the extra-large basin it fills than the three-piece mixer or monobloc fixture more commonly used with a smaller bowl.**

opposite, below right **The sculptural three-piece Starck basin mixer with lever handles from the Axor collection by Hansgrohe is well chosen for this console basin, carrying the eye along its width. Like all good designs it works well, the levers being easy to operate with dry or soapy hands.**

above left **Antique chrome faucets have a beautiful silvery patina, much softer than the bright gloss of new chrome. Modern finishes that come close to this are satinized chrome and nickel.**

above center **Salvaged antique bath faucets with their worn chrome finish unrestored are a quirky choice for this modern mosaic bathtub. Although external wear is unimportant, old faucets should only be bought if they are in full working order, as it is hard to find spare parts for them—and skilled engineers willing to repair them are even more elusive.**

above right **Antique faucets put the finishing touch to a traditional bathroom, and if you are lucky enough to have inherited them along with the original fixtures, they are worth preserving.**

center right **Strong, simple shapes strike the right note in a contemporary bathroom and few faucet designs are more pared-down than the Starck single-lever basin mixer from the Axor line by Hansgrohe. Understated and sculptural, it is specially designed for use on smaller basins.**

below right **Wall-mounted faucets have the advantage of leaving the basin rim clear so its shape can be properly appreciated and, more prosaically, it becomes easier to clean. These faucets, from the Tara range by Dornbracht, are a contemporary take on the traditional crosshead pattern.**

this page, above left **In this stylish limestone bathroom, ducting for the plumbing forms a narrow shelf for toiletries. The mirrored cabinets eliminate the need for a separate looking-glass and visually widen this narrow room.** this page, above right **A heated towel rod often produces enough heat to warm a small bathroom. The Cobratherm by Bisque is a close alternative to this serpentine chrome towel rod.** this page, center right **Wall-mounted glass accessories with chrome or brass fixtures are bathroom classics and therefore widely available. More difficult to source are ceramic accessories that form an integral part of the tiling. Longmead Ceramics is one of the few remaining makers.** this page, below right **Accessories like this chrome towel ring can be found in department stores.** opposite, above left **Freestanding cabinets are useful in a bathroom without enough built-in storage. The reflective surfaces of this piece by Lineabeta (widely available in department stores) are helpful in a small room.** opposite, above center **This glass and chrome wall-mounted O.L.C. rack by Agape keeps reading matter neat in the bathroom.** opposite, above right **This built-in storage combines cupboards and drawers in a single unit. The drawers pull right out for better access. The idea of aligning the cupboard handles and drawer pulls on one side is a design feature that distinguishes the piece from a store-bought cabinet.** opposite, below **Built-in furniture packs a lot of storage into a compact space. These cabinets were custommade in blond birch to match the furniture in the adjoining bedroom and raised on small chrome legs to give a less weighty look. The top, undermounted with a pair of Kohler basins, is made from luminous white Carrara marble.**

storage & accessories

Clutter has a tendency to accumulate in the bathroom, but accessories to hold items in everyday use, combined with well-planned storage for the things you want to display (and the things you would rather hide away) will keep it under control.

Floor-standing bathroom cupboards, wall cabinets, and storage trolleys can be found in furniture and department stores, but pieces intended for elsewhere in the house can be used just as well in the bathroom, provided they will not be damaged by the damp environment. Purpose-made built-in bathroom furniture is becoming more widely available in contemporary and classic styles. Constructed along similar lines to kitchen cabinets, they are sold in modular form so you can create an arrangement to fit your space. Custommade built-in furniture is usually created as part of a complete bathroom installation and can be designed as the main feature or cleverly concealed. Whatever the type of storage, in a family bathroom a lockable cupboard or compartment is important for the safe keeping of medicines and sharp items.

Toothbrushes and handtowels need to be kept within reach of where they will be used. For these, wall-mounted fixtures are ideal. Perfume bottles, spare soaps, and other items that are both decorative and frequently used can be arranged on open shelves.

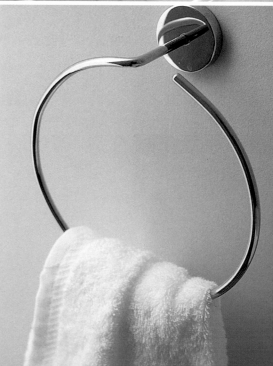

opposite, above left **Stone can be used successfully for virtually any bathroom surface. For pure elegance, choose pale stone with an interesting grain like this unfilled travertine.**
opposite, above center **Iroko (a hardwood that can tolerate some moisture) panels the wall behind this bathtub. Instead of conforming to the usual vertical pattern of wainscoting, a contemporary effect has been achieved by setting the planks horizontally and leaving regular narrow gaps between them.**

opposite, above right **Concrete is an unlikely choice for a sophisticated bathroom, but here a special mix devised by Unique Environments forms the lightly textured, water-resistant walls and smooth steps leading to a sunken bathtub.**
opposite, center left **Terrazzo covers the floor and continues up the sides of the tub in this traditional room.**
opposite, center **Caribbean Mix is the appropriate name for the multitoned blue mosaic tiles which line this shower area.**

opposite, center right **Smooth tiles and fine, gritty cement render provide textural contrast in this wet room.**
opposite, below left **Harvey Maria's cork-and-vinyl "Spring" tiles give the impression of a carpet of roses—a frivolous touch in a tiny bathroom.**
opposite, below center **Warm gray-brown mussel limestone has narrow, vertical grooves on its horizontal planes in contrast with the smooth, fossil-studded horizontal surfaces.**
opposite, below right **The contrast of fresh green mosaic tiles and the**

natural tones of wood and marble adds a lively note.
below left **These pearly iridescent mosaic tiles form a shimmering surface for a shower area. Similar tiles are available from Fired Earth.**
below center **Paint of the kind used to coat swimming pools waterproofs the walls of this shower room. Temachlor chlorinated rubber paint by Tikkurila Coatings can be colored to order.**
below right **Raw, robust waterproof cement render forms a continuous textured surface for the shower wall.**

surface finishes

If a bathroom is to stay looking good, all its surfaces must be moisture tolerant. Floors, shower areas, and basin counters should be impervious; but walls, furniture, and surfaces not in obviously wet areas need only resist occasional splashes of water and the humid atmosphere.

Ceramic tiles and mosaics are traditional surfaces for bathrooms. As long as the grouting is sound, they are completely waterproof and can be used to line a wet room, shower area, or even a built-in bathtub. Natural stone is a favorite for contemporary bathrooms, but to prevent watermarks it is advisable to protect it with a clear seal. Concrete is sometimes used as an alternative to stone. It can be waterproofed by adding the appropriate ingredient during installation and is sometimes surface sealed, too. Some tropical hardwoods, such as teak, can be used in wet areas. Other wood must be well coated with marine varnish, with joints sealed to prevent moisture penetration. Rubber and vinyl flooring have good water resistance and come in a choice of colors and designs, making them a practical and decorative choice.

DIRECTORY

a= above; b = below; c = center; l = left; r = right

DOORS & WINDOWS

general & miscellaneous

ECLECTICS
Contemporary window blinds in all styles and sliding panels for doorways
Tel: +44 1843 852888
www.eclectics.co.uk

FARROW & BALL
Traditional wallpapers and paints, including floor paint; international direct sales and stockists worldwide (See Flooring)

traditional & architectural joinery

ADVANCED EQUIPMENT CORPORATION
Operable walls similar to that featured pp 12–13
2401 W. Commonwealth Ave
Fullerton CA 92833
Tel: 714-635-5350
Fax: 714-525-6083
www.advancedequipment.com

SMOKE GUARD CORPORATION
Special smoke-proof doors
11420 Executive Drive
Boise ID 83713
Tel: 208-383-3789 or 800-574-0330
Fax: 208-344-8385
www.smokeguard.com

TOTAL DOORS BY OPENINGS INC.
Elegant doors with a unique full-vertical-length locking channel and hinge
40 West Howard
Pontiac MI 48342-1280
Tel: 248-335-7380
Fax: 248-335-6868
www.total-door.com

handles, pulls, & hardware

ALLGOOD WORLDWIDE
High-quality contemporary ironmongery
Tel: +44 870 609 0009
Fax: +44 20 7380 1232
www.allgood.com

HÄFELE
Huge range of cabinet and furniture ironmongery
www.hafele.com
Häfele America Co.
Archdale NC 27263
3901 Cheyenne Drive
POB 40 00
Tel: 336-889-2322
Fax: 336-431-3831
info_us@hafeleamericas.com
www.hafeleonline.com

MERIT METAL PRODUCTS
Excellent range of hardware
242 Valley Road
Warrington PA 18976
Tel: 215-343-2500
Fax: 215-343-4839
info@meritmetal.com
www.meritmetal.com

NU-LINE
London shop offering a good range of hardware
317 Westbourne Park Road
London W11 1EF, UK
Tel: +44 20 7727 7748
Fax: +44 20 7792 9451

PHOENIX LOCK COMPANY
Squash-court ring pull or flush ring pull
321 Third Avenue West
Newark NJ 07107-2392
Tel: 973-483-0976
Fax: 973-483-0977
www.phoenixlock.com

SATURN ARCHITECTURAL
Architectural ironmongery
Wellington Business Park
Crowthorn RG45 6LS, UK
Tel: +44 1344 761194
Fax: +44 1344 762467

VALLI & VALLI U.S.A. INC.
Designer door furniture
150 East 58th Street, 4th floor
New York NY 10155
Tel: 212-326-8811 or 877-326-2565
Fax: 212-326-8816
sales@vallivalli-us.com
www.vallievalli.com

WEINSTEIN & HOLTZMAN HARDWARE GROUP
Full range of door hardware
29 Park Row
New York NY 10038-2302
Tel: 212-233-4651
Fax: 212-571-5301
office@weholtzman.com
www.doorframesandhardware.com

windows & skylights

CRITTALL WINDOWS LTD
Steel windows and doors; will replicate period metal windows for restoration projects
info@crittallna.com
www.crittallna.com
Available from:
W L Hall Company
14800 Martin Drive
Eden Prairie MN 55344-2096
Tel: 952-937-8400
Fax: 952-937-9126
www.wlhall.com

FISHER SKYLIGHTS
Metal-framed skylights, from pre-designed modular systems to custom-engineered projects
5005 Veterans Memorial Highway
Holbrook NY 11741
Tel: 800-431-1586
Fax: 631-563-3399
www.fisherskylights.com

KALWALL
Wall systems, curtain walls, windows, standard skylights, pre-engineered and custom skylights, sloped glazing systems, plastic unit skylights, and translucent skylights
1111 Candia Road
PO Box 237
Manchester NH 03105
Tel: 603-627-3861 or 800-258-9777
Fax: 603-627-7905
www.kalwall.com
info@kalwall.com

METAL UK
Windows and conservatories
Tel: +44 1895 629940
Fax: +44 1895 678811
equiries@metaluk.co.uk
www.metaluk.co.uk

SUNFOLD SYSTEMS
Folding and sliding doors and automated rooflights
The Greenhouse
93 Norwich Road, East Dereham
Norfolk NR20 3AL, UK
Tel: +44 1362 699744
Fax: +44 1362 698787

VELUX AMERICA INC.
P.O. Box 5001
Greenwood SC 29648
Tel: 800-88-VELUX
www.velux-america.com

VISIONWALL CORPORATION
High-performance windows, curtain walls, and sloped glazing systems in clear, tinted, or reflective glass
17915-118 Avenue
Edmonton, Alberta
Canada T5S 1L6
Tel: 780-451-4000 or 800-400-8633
Fax: 780-451-4745
www.visionwall.com

WAUSAU WINDOW & WALL
Custommade windows and curtain walls, projected/casement windows, ribbon/strip windows, double- or single-hung, sliding doors, and horizontal sliders
1415 West Street
Wausau WI 54401
Tel: 715-845-2161 or 877-678-2983
Fax: 715-843-4055
www.wausauwindows.com

WESTCROWNS INC.
Pilkington profilit translucent linear glazing system for walls or windows
P.O. Box 7913
Shallotte NC 28470
Tel: 910-579-4441
Fax: 910-575-3203
www.westcrowns.com

FLOORING

general

FARROW & BALL INC
Contact for direct sales or your nearest stockist
Tel: 845-369-4912
usasales@farrow-ball.com
Farrow & Ball (Canada)
1054 Yonge Street
Toronto, Ontario
Tel: 416-920-0200
fandb@istar.com
www.farrow-ball.com

MASONRY CONTRACTORS ASSOCIATION OF AMERICA
Provides directory of members, informational publications, and building advice
1910 South Highland Avenue
Suite 101
Lombard IL 60148
www.masonryshowcase.com

NATIONAL CONSTRUCTION ESTIMATOR
The quickest, easiest way to find labor and material cost estimates for nearly any residential, commercial or industrial construction project
www.get-a-quote.net

SPECIALTY COATINGS INC.
Specially formulated and patented epoxy resins make it three-times more durable than conventional paints such as enamels and urethanes in a wide variety of colors and shades, they will also match to Benjamin Moore swatches
784 Morris Tpk., Suite 316
Short Hills NJ 07078
Tel: 888-755-7361
www.armorpoxy.com

YOUR COMPLETE HOME
Provides listings for contractors in every state, as well as helpful information about financing, hiring, and do-it-yourself projects
www.yourcompletehome.com

hard flooring

ADVANCE TERRAZZO INC.
With over 50 marble, glass, and plastic aggregates, they can match any paint coloring when laying chips in resin flooring, or create specific mosaic designs
1217 East Gibson Lane
Phoenix AZ 85034
Tel: 800-323-9736 or 602-253-9400
www.advanceterrazzo.com

AMERICAN SLATE COMPANY
Experts in slate offering flooring products as well as technical assistance to professionals and homeowners alike
814 N. La Cienega Blvd.
Los Angeles CA
Tel: 800-553-5611
www.americanslate.com

ART TILE
Suppliers of a beautiful selection of Mexican Talavera, Spanish Valencian, Spanish Sevillian, Moorish, English Victorian and California-Malibu ceramic tiles
2410 North Main Avenue
San Antonio TX 78212
Tel: 888-735-TILE or 210-734-TILE
www.arttile.com

THE DURABAK COMPANY
Durabak™ is a specially formulated polyurethane slip-resistant concrete floor paint, truck bed liner, marine deck and safety coating
4064 S. Atchison Way, Suite 301
Aurora CO 80014
Tel: 303-690-7190
www.nonslipcoating.com

ECHEGUREN SLATE
Supplies African, American, Chinese, Indian Slate, as well as Brazilian Black, Grey, Green, Multicolor, and Purple
1495 Illinois Street
San Francisco CA 94107
Tel: 415-206-9343
www.echeguren.com

EMERY & CIE & NOIR D'IVOIRE
Rue de l'Hopital 25–29
Brussels
Belgium
Tel: +32 2513 5892
gabi.emery@euronet.be

FIRED EARTH
Tiles, wood flooring, natural flooring, rugs, plus bathrooms; call for export sales
Tel: +44 1295 814316
export@firedearth.com
www.firedearth.com

GRANITE & MARBLE INTERNATIONAL LTD
Supply and installation of natural stone; for floors, walls, countertops, basins
Tel: +44 20 7498 2742
sales@stonework.co.uk
stonework.co.uk

GRATING PACIFIC INC.
Metal industrial flooring
3651 Sausalito Street
Los Alamitos CA 90720
Tel: 800-321-4314
www.gratingpacific.com

LUXOMATION LTD
Stainless-steel tiles
Tel: +44 20 8568 6373
www.luxomation.com

PARIS CERAMICS
Limestone, stone and terracotta floors, mosaics
150 East 58th Street, 7th Floor
New York NY 10155
Tel: 212-644-2782
www.parisceramics.com

STEVE CHARLES LTD
Tile, stone, marble, mosaic and pebble for floors and walls manufactured and exported internationally
E1, The Engineering Offices
2 Michael Road
London SW6 2AD, UK
Tel: +44 20 7384 4424
sales.stevecharles.com
www.stevecharles.com

STONE LOCATOR
Search-engine service provided by Castle Distributors Inc. enables users to research, locate, and purchase natural stone products such as marble, granite, limestone, travertine, slate and mosaics as well as ceramic, porcelain, and precast products
2111 Wilson Blvd., Suite 700
Arlington VA 22201
Tel: 703-516-6690
www.stonelocator.com

VILLEROY & BOCH AG
P.O. Box 1120
D - 66688 Mettlach
Germany
Tel: +49 6864-81-0
www.villeroy-boch.com

wooden flooring
ACCESS FLOOR SYSTEMS, INC.
Complete systems and kits for raised panel flooring
P.O. Box 1148
Abita Springs LA 70420
Tel: 800-868-8606
www.accessfloor.com

JUNCKERS INDUSTRIER A/S
Værttsvej
DK-4600 Køge
Denmark
Tel: + 45 5665 1895
junckers@junckers.dk
www.junckers.com
Junckers Hardwood, Inc.
4920 E. Landon Drive
Anaheim CA 92807
Tel: 800-878-9663 or 714-777-6430
information@junckershardwood.com
www.junckershardwood.com

KINGSPAN ACCESS FLOORS LTD
Access floors
Tel: +44 1482 781701
mail@kingspan.co.uk for all worldwide enquiries
www.kingspanaccessfloors.co.uk

MAFI HOLZVERARBEITUNG GMBH
A-5212 Schneegattern 7
Austria
Tel: +43 7746 2711
office@mafi.at
www.mafi.co.at
Mafi Wide Plank Floors, Inc.
9702 Gayton Rd, PMB 291
Richmond VA 23233
Tel: 804-754-1815
pezet@mafiwideplankfloors.com

ROBBINS HARDWOOD FLOORS
Canadian maple strip and Canadian maple plank floors; contact for locations throughout U.S.
16803 Dallas Parkway
Addison TX 75001
Tel: 800-733-3309
www.armstrong.com/resrobbinsna

THE SUMMER BEAM COMPANY
Salvagers, restorers, and suppliers of historic wood and architectural antiques
Seattle Building Salvage
330 Westlake Ave. N.
Seattle WA
Tel: 206-381-3453
www.thesummerbeam.com

THOMAS D. OSBORNE MOSAIC HARDWOOD FLOORS
Specializing in custom design, fabrication and installation of commissioned marquet and inlaid floors using native and exotic hardwoods
1421 Northampton Street
Holyoke MA 01040
Tel: 413-532-9034
www.thefloorist.com

TURKSTRA LUMBER
Spruce plywood flooring
4555 Kent Street
Niagara Falls ON
Canada L2H 1J1
Tel: 905-374-0176
www.turkstralumber.com

UPM-KYMMENE WOOD PRODUCTS INDUSTRY
Wisa wood
P.O. Box 380
00101 Helsinki
Finland
Tel: +358 204 15 111

sheet & soft tile
BILL AMBERG
230 Elizabeth Street
New York NY 10012
Tel: 212-625-8556
www.billamberg.com

BLACKSTOCK LEATHER
13452 Kennedy Road
Stouffville, Ontario
L4A 7X5 Canada
Tel: 905-888-7070 or 800-663-6657
info@blackstockleather.com
www.blackstockleather.com

CLASSIC TILE INC.
Installers and distributors of Estrie and Flexco textured rubber flooring, as well as Anderson hardwood, Congoleum, Formica, Wicander vinyl-clad cork, poured rubber floors, and many other quality resilient flooring surfaces
325 Pine Street
Elizabeth NJ 07206
Tel: 908-289-8400
www.classictile.com

DALSOUPLE
Rubber floors and other surfaces, exported internationally
PO Box 140, Bridgwater
Somerset TA5 1HT, UK
Tel: +44 1984 667233
info@dalsouple.com
www.dalsouple.com

FORBO INTERNATIONAL SA
Marmoleum and cushioned vinyl
8193 Eglisau
Zurich, Switzerland
Tel: +41 1 868 2525
info@forbo.com
www.forbo.com
Forbo linoleum Inc.
Humboldt Industrial Park
P.O. Box 667
Hazleton PA 18201
Tel: 570-459-0771
information@forbo-industries.com
www.forbo-industries.com

TREADMASTER
Anti-slip flooring in rubber-bonded cork; visit online store
Lewmar Marine
2050 34th Way #B
Largo FL33771
Tel: 727-538-5600
www.theoutdoorscenter.com

natural fibers & carpets
CENTRO
Stock Christine Vanderhurd rugs
4729 Mc Pherson Avenue
St. Louis MO98101
Tel: 314-454-0111
Fax: 314-454-0112
www.centro-inc.com

CHRISTINE VANDERHURD
Custom-designed handwoven, machine-made, and tufted rugs and carpets
www.christinevanderhurd.com

CHRISTOPHER FARR
Handmade contemporary rugs
Courtyard Gallery
748 N. La Cienega Blvd.
Los Angeles CA 90069
Tel: 310 967 0064
Fax: 310-967-0065
info@christopherfarrdesigns.com
www.cfarr.co.uk

DIMENSIONS NOUVELLE
Contemporary rugs including designs by Helen Yardley
3900 NE First Avenue
Maimi FL 33137
Tel: 305-573-7711
www.dimensionrug.com

HELEN YARDLEY
Hand-tufted rugs and wall hangings
A/Z Studios, 3/5 Hardwidge Street
London SE1 3SY, UK
Tel: +44 20 7403 7114
info@helenyardley.com
www.helenyardley.com

HENDRICKSEN NATÜRLICH
Specializes in creating interiors with environmentally safe and durable materials, including natural-fiber rugs and natural linoleum flooring
PO Box 1677
Sebastopol CA 95473-1677
Tel: 707-824-0914

ROGER OATES DESIGN
Rugs and runners in contemporary designs, textured finishes, neutral flatweave and Wiltons; contact for your nearest dealer
Tel: +44 1531 631611
shop@rogeroates.com
www.rogeroates.com

STARK CARPETS
Carpets and rugs
D&D Building
979 Third Avenue, 11th Floor
New York NY 10022-1276
Tel: 212-752-9000
info@starkcarpet.com
www.starkcarpet.com

WALLS & CEILINGS
(See Doors & Windows for traditional
& architectural joinery)

ALL-RITE DOCK & DOOR SYSTEMS INC
*PVC strip-curtain door system for
attaching panels of leather*
52 Van Kirk Drive
Brampton ON L7A 1B1
Canada
Tel: 905-840-4848
www.all-ritedoors.com/p_v_c.htm

ARMOURCOAT SURFACE FINISHES
Decorative polished plaster finishes
www.armourcoat.com
US Distributor:
Symmetry Products Group
117 Douglas Avenue
Providence RI 02904
Tel: 800-886-3626

BILHUBER BASICS
Bilhuber Inc.
3330 East 59th Street, 6th Floor
New York NY 10022
Tel: 212-308-4888

BUTLER MANUFACTURING COMPANY
*Manufacturers of "intelligent"
electro-polarizing glass*
1540 Genessee
Kansas City MO 64102
Tel: 816-968-3000
www.butlermfg.com

CHARLESTON MARBLE & GRANITE
*Marble suppliers, including suppliers
of travertine wall panels*
2770 Maybank Highway, Suite G
Johns Island SC 29455
Tel: 843-559-8055
www.charlestonmarbleandgranite.com

GRAHAM & BROWN INC.
Textured wallpapers
3 Corporate Drive
Cranbury NJ 08512
Tel: 609-395-9200
Fax: 609-395-9676
pspringman@grahambrownusa.com
www.grahambrown.com

THE INTERNATIONAL MASONRY INSTITUTE
*Central body to find builders to, for
example, grit-blast a wall or seal a
concrete ceiling*
The James Brice House
42 East Street
Annapolis MD 21401
Tel: 410-280-1305
www.imiweb.org/imihome.htm

THE INTERNET WALLPAPER STORE
3-D textured wallpapers
Tamarak Development Group
23822 W. Valencia Blvd, Suite 310
Valencia CA 91355
Tel: 877-255-0907 or 661-255-0907

MWEMBELA TIMBER COMPANY
African hardwoods, including iroko
Tel: 312-617-6002

NORTH AMERICAN WHOLESALE LUMBER ASSOCIATION
Central body of timber suppliers
3601 Algonquin Road, Suite 400
Rolling Meadows IL 60008
Tel: 847-870-7470
www.lumber.org

OAKWOOD VENEER COMPANY
*Suppliers of exotic veneers of wood
paneling walls, including sapele
pomelle and burl oak*
3642 W. 11 Mile Road
Berkley MI 48072
Tel: 800-426-6018 or 248-542-9979
www.oakwoodveneer.com

PAPERS & PAINTS
*Paint specialist with excellent range
of historical colours and off whites;
offer international mail-order service*
4 Park Walk
London SW10 0AD, UK
Tel: +44 20 7352 8626
Fax: +44 20 7352 1017
enquiries@papers-paints.co.uk
www.papers-paints.co.uk

PITTSBURGH CORNING CORPORATION
*Manufacturers of clear and
translucent glass bricks for walls
(internal and external)*
800 Presque Isle Drive
Pittsburgh PA 15239
Tel: 724-327-6100
www.pittsburghcorning.com

PLYMOUTH QUARRIES
*Suppliers of over 100 varieties of
stone and 50 varieties of brick*
410 Whiting Street (Rte. 53)

Hingham MA 02043
Tel: 781-335-3686
www.plymouthquarries.com

PRIVA-LITE
Electrically switchable obscured glass
www.sggprivalite.com

PROVIDENCE INTERNATIONAL
African hardwoods, including iroko
Tel: 570-476-5571

SOLARIS GLASS BRICKS
Siemensstraße 1
D-56422 Wirges
Germany
Tel: +49 2602 681-0
Fax: +49 2602 681-425
info.solaris-glasstein@saint-gobain.com
info-export.solaris-glasstein@saint-gobain.com
www.solaris-glasstein.de

TIMOROUS BEASTIES
*Wallcoverings including bespoke and
Op-art designs*
7 Craigend Place
Glasgow G13 2UN, UK
Tel: + 44 141 959 3331
Fax: + 44 141 959 8880
www.timorousbeasties.com

VINCI STONE PRODUCTS
*Suppliers of Idaho Quartzite honey
ledgestone*
798 Marriotsville Road
Mariottsville MD 21104
Tel: 410-442-1460
www.vincistone.com

VINTAGE BEAMS AND TIMBERS
*Suppliers of reclaimed traditional
wooden paneling*
P O Box 548
Sylva NC 28779
Tel: 828-586-0755
www.vintagebeamsandtimbers.com

STAIRCASES
(See Doors & Windows for traditional
& architectural joinery)

ALLEN ASSOCIATES
*General contractors with experience
in concrete staircase design*
1427 Tunnel Road
Santa Barbara CA 93105
Tel: 805-682-4305
www.dennisallenassociates.com

ARCWAYS
*Builders of custom curved and spiral
staircases*
P.O. Box 763
Neenah WI 54957
Tel: 800-558-5096
Fax: 920-725-2053

CURVOFLITE STAIRS AND MILLWORK
*Supplier of architectural millwork,
including stairs (circular and spiral),
raised paneling, doors, and kitchen
cabinets*
205 Spencer Avenue
Chelsea MA 02150
Tel: 617-889-0007
Fax: 617-889-6339
www.curvoflite.com

CUSTOM HARDWOODS, LLC
*High-end stair parts and pre-built
staircases in wood and iron*
673 Park Avenue
Genoa IL 60135
Tel: 815-784-9974
Fax: 815-784-8459
www.stair-parts.com

D.S. NELSON CO. INC.
*Custom stairbuilders in wood, glass,
or metal*
115 Airport Street
North Kingston RI 02852
Tel: 401-267-1000
Fax: 401-295-4756
www.dsnelson.com

JAMES CARPENTER DESIGN ASSOCIATES
Designers of glass staircases
145 Hudson Street
New York NY 10013
212-431-4318

SALTER INDUSTRIES
*Steel, aluminum, and solid wood
spiral stairs*
105 GP Clement Drive
Collegeville PA 19426
Tel: 800-368-8280 or 610-489-5799
www.salterspiralstair.com

SHOWER DOOR OF CANADA
*Specialty glass staircases, railings,
and bent glass*
Dufferin Business Centre
2700 Dufferin Street, Unit 70
Toronto, Ontario
Canada M6B 4J3
Tel: 416-781-9833 or 877-781-9833
Fax: 416-781-9959
www.showerdoorcanada.com

HEATING

general & miscellaneous
AMERICAN SOCIETY OF HEATING,
REFRIGERATION AND AIR
CONDITIONING ENGINEERS INC.
17191 Tullie Circle NE
Atlanta GA 30329-3025
Tel: 404-636-8400
www.ashrae.org

ENERGY EFFICIENCY & RENEWABLE ENERGY CLEARINGHOUSE (EREC)
P.O. Box 3048
Merrifield VA 22116-0121
Tel: 800-363-3732
www.eren.doe.gov

GAROUSTE & BONETTI AT DAVID GILL GALLERIES
Contemporary decorative furniture
60 Fulham Road
London SW3 6HH, UK
Tel: +44 20 7589 5946
Fax: +44 20 7584 9184
info@davidgillgalleries.co.uk

TO LOCATE LOCAL HEATING
PROFESSIONALS NEAR YOU:
www.acdoctor.com

UNITED GROUP, INC.
*Distributors of Widney telescopic
slides*
13700 Polo Trail Drive
Lake Forest IL 60045
Tel: 800-223-7003
www.unitedgp.com

fireplaces, surrounds, & grates
ARCHITECTURAL SALVAGE, W.D. INC.
*Original and reproduction antique
architectural details including
mantles and fireplace accessories*
614–618 East Broadway
Louisville KY 40202
Tel: 502-589-0670
www.architecturalsalvage.com

THE ARTS & CRAFTS SOCIETY
*Listings of resources for Arts and
Crafts products*
1194 Bandera Drive
Ann Arbor MI 48103
Tel: 734-665-4729
www.arts-crafts.com

CHESNEY'S
Antique and new fireplaces in marble, stone, and wood and a range of grates
Suite 244, 2nd Floor
D&D Building
979 Third Avenue
New York
Tel: 646-840-0609
www.antiquefireplace.co.uk

COMFORT GLOW HEATING PRODUCTS
Fire boxes, inset fireplaces, radiant flame heaters, and much more
1251 Mound Ave.
Grand Rapids MI. 49504
Tel: 616-791-7325
www.comfortglow.com

CVO FIREVAULTS
Range of contemporary gas fires and special commissions
36 Great Titchfield Street
London W1P 7AD, UK
Tel: +44 20 7580 5333
Fax: +44 20 7255 2234
info@cvo.co.uk
www.cvo.co.uk

THE FIREPLACE SHOP
Andirons and firedogs
379 Eglinton Avenue West
Toronto, Canada M5N 1A3
www.thefireplaceshop.com

GAZCO LTD
British manufacturers of flame-effect gas fires and stoves including modern inset and Victorian reproduction fireplaces; also offer made-to-measure service
Tel: +44 1392 444030
Fax +44 1392 444148
info@gazco.com
www.gazco.com

KAREN MICHELLE ANTIQUE TILES
Antiques art tiles and fire surrounds
P.O. Box 489
Bridgewater CT 06752
Tel: 860-354-7197

OLDE WORLD CABINETRY, INC.
Great source for turn-of-the century antique wood mantles
Tel: 303-736-4378
www.antiquemantles.com

PLATONIC FIREPLACE COMPANY
Produce unusual contemporary flame-effect gas fires with ceramic "Geolog" 3-dimensional shapes, pebbles and rocks instead of coals,

similar to the fire featured on p92
Phoenix Wharf
Eel Pie Island, Twickenham
Middlesex TW1 3DY, UK
Tel: +44 20 8891 5904
Fax +44 20 8892 2590
platonicfireplace@btinternet.com
www.platonicfireplaces.co.uk

VINCI STONE PRODUCTS, INC.
Stone masons for fireplace, kitchen, bathroom, and landscaping projects
(See Walls & Ceilings)

radiators & heating systems

A-1 NEW & USED
Great source of salvage radiators
30 Prospect Street
Somerville MA 02143-3419
Tel: 617-625-6140

ACTION SUPPLY COMPANY
Designer bathroom, kitchen, and plumbing fixtures
4210 So. Military Trail
Lake Worth FL 33461
Tel: 561-964-4700 or 866-2FAUCET
www.actionsupply.com

BISQUE
(See Bathrooms)

CLYDE COMBUSTIONS LTD
Column and tubular steel radiators and towel rails
Tel: +44 20 8391 2020
Fax: +44 20 8397 4598
www.clyde4heat.co.uk

GUNNING ENGINEERING LTD
British manufacturer of tubular radiators, trench heating, and grilles
Tel: +44 70 41 351 313
www.gunning-heating-products.co.uk

HOWELL
Cast-iron sectional radiators of all sizes and styles, seat radiators, die-cast aluminum radiators, and Arco cast-iron column radiators
119 E. King Street
P.O. Box 1673
Johnson City TN 37605-1673
Tel: 423-929-8548
www.hydronics.com

JAGA INTERNATIONAL
Belgian manufacturer of trench heaters, tubular, panel radiators, and bathroom radiators
Tel: +32 11 29 41 16
e-mail: sales@jaga.be
www.theradiatorfactory.com

JUST OPTIONS
Wide selection of towel-rail and column radiators
633 Langdale Dr.
Ft. Collins CO 80526-3941
Tel: 970-266-1907
www.just-options.com

MOR ELECTRIC HEATING ASSOC., INC. & INFRARED INTERNATIONALE OF NORTH AMERICA, LTD.
Ceramic, panel, infrared, and quartz heaters
5880 Alpine Ave. NW
Comstock Park MI 49321
Tel: 616-784-1121 or 800 442-2581
www.infraredheaters.com

RADIANT ELECTRIC HEAT, INC.
Ceramic radiant heaters, including baseboard, ceiling, and portable; also short columns of varying lengths
3695 North 126th Street – Unit N
Brookfield, Wisconsin 53005
Tel: 262-783-1282 or 800-774-4450
www.electricheat.com

SA THERMIC NV/AG/PLC
Horizontal and vertical rail radiators
Heulentakstraat 2/n
B-3650 Dilsen, Belgium
Tel: +32 89/790444
Fax: +32 89/790555
www.thermic.be

ZEHNDER
Column and panel radiators and towel rails
Moortalstrasse 1
Postfach, CH-5722 Gränichen
Switzerland
Tel: +41 62 855 15 00
info@zehnder.net
US distributor:
Runtal North America, Inc.
187 Neck Road
PO Box 8278, Ward Hill MA 01835
Tel: 978-373-1666
www.runtalnorthamerica.com

stoves

AUSTROFLAMM INDUSTRIES, INC.
American distributors of the RIKA wood-burning stove
1007 International Drive
Oakdale PA 15071
Tel: 724-695-2430
www.austroflammus.com

ESSE
Heating and cooking stoves; matt-black and enamelled stoves including some reproduction Art Nouveau designs; models similar to that

featured p102 al
Ouzledale Foundry Co Ltd
esse@ouzledale.co.uk
www.ouzledale.co.uk

GOOD TIME STOVE CO.
Wide selection of antique wood-burning and multi-fuel stoves, including cylinder stoves
Box 306, Route 112
Goshen MA 01032-0306
Tel: 888-282-7506
www.goodtimestove.com

MORSØ
Scandinavian cast-iron stoves
Furvej 9, 7900 Nykøbing Mors
Denmark
Tel: +45 9669 1900
email: stoves@morsoe.com
www.morsoe.com
US Distributors:
Hearthlink International
9 Maple Street
Randolph VT05060
Tel: 802 728 9342
jrking@adelphia.net
Miles Industries Inc.
829 West Third Street
North Vancouver BC V7P 3K7
Tel: 604-984-3496
mmiles@valorflame.com

RAIS ART OF FIRE
Wood burning and multi-fuel stoves
Industrivej 20, Vangen
DK-9900 Frederikshaven,
Denmark
www.rais.dk

STOVES UNLIMITED
Over 25 different varieties of free-standing wood-burning stoves
P.O. Box 1233
Verndale, WA 99037
Tel: 888-470-7011
www.stovesunlimited.com

VERMONT CASTINGS
410 Admiral Boulevard
Mississauga
Ontario L5T 2N6
Canada
Tel: 800-227-8683
www.vermontcastings.com
Call for nearest dealer

YEOMAN STOVES
Cylinder stoves similar to that featured p102al
Tel: +44 13952 34567
Fax: +44 1395 234568
sales@yeoman-stoves.co.uk
www.yeoman-stoves.co.uk

STORAGE

ARMANI CASA SOHO
Christian Biecher is the designer for the new Armani Casa collection
97 Greene Street
New York, NY 10012
Tel: 212-334-1271
www.armanicasa.com

CLOSET FACTORY
Complete customization, each piece is designed and built to order
9400-A West, Robinson Road
Franklin Park IL 60131
Tel: 800-464-7678 or 847-928-2100
www.closetfactory.com

CLOSET & STORAGE CONCEPTS
Designs and installs custom storage systems for closets, garages, offices, pantries, and entertainment centers in a variety of styles
424 Commerce Lane
West Berlin NJ 08091
Tel: 888-THE-CLOSET or 856-767-5700
www.closetandstorageconcepts.com

GLAVERBEL
www.glaverbel.com
US Distributor:
James E. Berrigan
PO Box 6834
Metairie LA70009
Tel: 504-888-7947
jebinc6834@aol.com

HOLLY HUNT
Supplier of Christain Liagre wall sconces featured p110b
150 E 58th Street
New York NY10155
Tel 212 891 2500
Fax 212 891 2599
www.hollyhunt.com

IKEA
Tel: 847-969-9700 or 800-434-4532
www.ikea-usa.com

IMPROVENET INC.
Screens and recommends quality contractors and architects for every kind of remodeling and storage design job
1286 Oddstad Drive
Redwood City CA 94063
Tel: 877-517-2928
www.improvenet.com

INTERLÜBKE
Sleek contemporary storage for bedrooms and living rooms
Gebr. Lubke GmbH & Co KG
D-33378 Rheda-Widenbruck
Germany
Tel: +49 52 42/12-1
Fax: +49 52 42/12-206
www.interluebke.de

LIGNE ROSET
Contemporary furnishings
(See Lighting)

MOSS
Stockists of Vitsoe shelving
146 Greene Street
New York NY10012
Tel: 212-226-2190
Fax: 212-226-8473
www.mossonline.com

NATIONAL CLOSET GROUP
Provides a network of the best independent storage design companies in the country
953 North Larch
Elmhurst IL 60126
Tel: 866-624-5463
www.nationalclosetgroup.com

NEOTU
Design company featuring furniture designed by Christian Biecher
545 W34 Street, Suite 3C
New York NY10001
Tel: 212-695-9404
neotunyc@neotu.com
www.neotu.com

PUNT MOBLES S.L.
Maker of the Literatura shelving system
Islas Baleares, 48
46988 Fuente del Jarro
Valencia, Spain
Tel: +34 96 1343270
Fax: +34 96 134268
puntmobles@puntmobles.es
www.puntmobles.es

VITSOE
Classic 20th-century modern shelving; distribute internationally from London offices
Tel: +44 20 7354 8444
Fax: +44 20 7354 9888
details@vitsoe.com
www.vitsoe.com

LIGHTING

AF LIGHTING
Recessed spotlights
1310 Park Central Blvd S
Pompano Bch FL 33064
Tel: 954-972-5013 or 800-881-5483
Fax: 954-973-7457
nina@floridalighting.net

ANGLEPOISE
Tel: +44 1527 63771
Fax: +44 1527 61232
sales@anglepoise.co.uk
www.anglepoise.co.uk

ARTELUCE
(See Flos)

ARTEMIDE INC.
1980 New Highway
Farmingdale NY 11735
Tel: 631-694-9292
Fax: 631-694-9275
artemide_us@artemide.com
www.artemide.com

BEST & LLOYD
Traditional brass lighting, and "Bestlite" range
www.bestandlloyd.co.uk
US Distributor:
Luis Baldinger & Sons Inc.
19-02 Steinway
Long Island City NY 11105
Tel: 718-204-5700

BOX PRODUCTS LTD
Design and production of lighting, furniture and clocks to architects, interior designers and private clients
3 Russell House
Cambridge Street
London SW1V 4EQ, UK
Tel: +44 20 7401 2288
Fax: +44 20 7828 7133
boxproducts@btinternet.com

BOYD LIGHTING
944 Folsom Street
San Francisco CA 94107-1007
Tel: 415-778-4300 x345
Fax: 415-778-4319
info@boydlighting.com
www.boydlighting.com

CHARLOTTE PACKE
Lighting consultant and designer, one-off designs and some retail
C.P.D.
26 A The Avenue
London NW6 7YD
charlottepacke@yahoo.co.uk

CHRISTOPHER WRAY LIGHTING
591–593 Kings Road
London SW6 2YW, UK
Tel: +44 20 7751 8703
Fax: +44 20 7751 8704
www.christopherwray.co.uk

THE CONRAN SHOP
Furniture shops with good contemporary lighting
407 E 59th Street
New York NY 10022
Tel: 212-755-9079
Fax: 212-888-3008
www.conran.com

DAVID GILL GALLERIES
20th-century and contemporary furniture; Serge Mouille lighting
(See Heating)

ERCO LEUCHTEN GMBH
Brockhauser Weg 80-82
D-58507 Lüdenscheid
Tel: +49 2351 551 0
Fax: +49 2351 551 300
info@erco.com
www.erco.com

FC LIGHTING MANUFACTURERS INC.
Architectural downlighting, track, exterior, interior, and specialty lighting
1152 North Main Street
Lombard IL 60148-4804
Tel: 800-900-1730
Fax: 630-889-8106
www.fclighting.com

FLOS INC.
200 McKay Road
Huntington Station NY 11746
Tel: 631-549-2745
Fax: 631-549-2746
www.flos.net

FORBES & LOMAX LTD
Tel: +44 20 7738 0202
Fax: +44 20 7738 9224
sales@forbesandlomax.co.uk
www.forbesandlomax.co.uk

4 DESK TABLE LAMPS AND SHADES
Reproduction lighting in Art Nouveau and Tiffany styles
POB 25
Stewartsville NJ 08886
Tel: 908-479-4614
Fax: 908-479-6158
lamps@4-collectors.com
www.timelesslamps.com

HECTOR FINCH LIGHTING
Excellent range of of period and reproduction decorative lighting from 1900 to present day
88–90 Wandsworth Bridge Road
London SW6 2TF, UK
Tel: +44 20 7731 8886
Fax: +44 20 7731 7408
hector@hectorfinch.com
www.hectorfinch.com

HISTORIC LIGHTING INC
Wide range of Arts and Crafts lighting
114 East Lemon Avenue
Monrovia CA 91016
Tel: 626-303-4899
Fax: 626-358-6159
www.historiclighting.com

HOLOPHANE COMPANY INC.
25 South Park Place
P.O. Box 3004
Newark OH 43058
Tel: 740-345-9631
www.holophane.com

HOMEIER KUCHENTECHNIK GMBH
Kitchen extractors and lighting
Lichtenfelser Strasse 9
93057 Regensburg, Germany
Tel: +44 941 69 68 30
hreinhold@homeier.com
www.homeier.com

IGUZZINI ILLUMINAZIONE S.R.L.
s.s.77.Km102
62019 Recanati-MC, Italy
Tel: +39 071 758 81
Fax: +39 071 758 8295
iguzzini@iguzzi.it
www.iguzzini.com

IMPERIAL CAL PRODUCTS INC.
Under-hood lighting for kitchen countertops
1141 S. Acacia Avenue
Fullerton CA 92831
Tel: 714-446-7440
Fax: 714-446-7444
www.imperialhoods.com

IKEA
(See Storage)

INFORM
Lighting from Artemide and Flos; bathroom fixtures from Agape
1220 Western Avenue
Seattle WA 98101
Tel: 206 622 1608
www.informinteriors.com

ISAMU NOGUCHI GARDEN MUSEUM STORE
36-01 43rd Avenue at 36th Street
Long Island City
Queens NY 11101
Tel: 718-204-7088
Fax: 718-278-2348
www.noguchi.org

JOHN CULLEN LIGHTING
Discreet lighting for the house and garden
585 Kings Road
London SW6 2EH, UK
Tel: +44 20 7371 5400
Fax: +44 20 7371 7799
sales@johncullenlighting.co.uk
www.johncullenlighting.co.uk

KNOLL
Beautiful selection of modern and ergonomic desk lamps from original designers
1235 Water Street
East Greenville PA 18041
Tel: 800-343-5665
www.knoll.com

LIGHTING COLLABORATIVE
Suppliers of Electro Track
124 West 24th
New York NY 10011
Tel: 212-627-5330

LIGNE ROSET
Furnishing and lighting, including the Nelly lamp which is similar in design to the Whizz lamp featured p131a
250 Park Avenue
New York NY 10003
800-BY-ROSET
www.ligne-roset-usa.com

LIMN
Stylish contemporary furnishings including a good selection of lighting
290 Townsend Street
San Francisco CA 94107
Tel: 415-543-5466
Fax: 415-543-5971
sales@limn.com
www.limn.com

LOUIS POULSEN
Contemporary and modern classic lighting by Poul Heningsen, Arne Jacobsen, Verner Panton, and others
Nyhavn 11
Postboks 7, 1001 Kobenhavn K
Denmark
Tel: +45 33 14 14 114
Fax: +45 33 14 17 10
www.louis-poulsen.dk

Louis Poulsen Lighting, Inc.
3260 Meridan Parkway
Fort Lauderdale FL 33331
Tel: 954-349-2525
Fax: 954-349-2550
info@louispoulsen.com
www.louispoulsen.com

LUMESS AG
Contemporary light fittings
Binningerstrasse 101
4123 Allschwil
Switzerland
Tel: +41 61 481 0066
Fax: +41 61 481 9929

LUMINAIRE
*Stylish contemporary furnishings
including a good selection of
lighting; stores in Chicago and Miami*
Tel: 305-448-7367
Fax: 305-448-9447
www.luminaire.com

LUTRON ELECTRONICS CO.
Lighting controls
7200 Suter Road
Coopersburg PA18036
Tel: 610-282-3800
product@lutron.com
www.lutron.com

MATHMOS
*Lava lamps and other innovative
lighting*
US Sales:
Tel: +44 20 7549 2759
Fax: +44 20 7549 2715
us-support@mathmos.com
www.mathmos.com

MAX WATT DESIGN
*Contemporary wooden lamps and
shades in grasscloth, cork, and wood
veneer*
Tel/fax: +44 1508 532545

THE MICA LIGHT COMPANY
Reproduction Arts and Crafts lamps
517 State Street
Glendale CA 91203
Tel: 818-241-7227
Fax: 818-241-5839
sales@micalamps.com
www.micalamps.com

MOMA DESIGN STORE
*Classic designs for the home
including a good selection of lighting*
44 West 53rd Street
New York NY 10022
Tel: 800-447-6662
www.momastore.org

OPTELMA LIGHTING
*Low-voltage track lighting and
mains-voltage fittings*
Tel: +44 1235 553769
Fax: +44 1235 523005
sales@optelma.co.uk
www.optelma.co.uk

PACIFIC BURL & HARDWOOD
Wood veneer lampshades
6790 Williams Highway
Grants Pass OR 97527
Tel: 541-479-1854
bigred@budget.net

PHILIPS LIGHTING
200 Franklin Square Drive
Somerset NJ 08875
Tel: 800-555-0050
www.lighting.philips.com

RETROMODERN.COM
*Wonderful selection of over
180 of the best modern lamps*
805 Peachtree Street
Atlanta GA 30308
Tel: 877-724-0093
www.retromodern.com

SKK
*Innovative lighting consultants and
designers of fittings and switches*
34 Lexington Street
London W1F 0LH, UK
Tel: +44 20 7434 4095
Fax: +44 20 7287 0168
skk@easynet.co.uk
www.skk.net

STICTLY MISSION
17 East Third Street
Bethlehem City PA 18015
Tel: 610-814-3065 or 866-MISSION
www.strictlymission.com

TALLER UNO SA
*Range of contemporary table, floor,
wall, and hanging lights*
Balmes 11, 17465 Camallera
Girona, Spain
Tel: +34 972 79 41 27
Fax: +34 972 79 43 13
info@talleruno.com
www.talleruno.com
US Distributor:
Global Lighting
50 South Buckhout Street
Irvington NY 10533
Tel: 914-5914095
Fax: 914-5913796
info@globallighting.net

UNIQUE INTERIEUR
Kalkbrænderiløbskaj 4
dk-2100 Copenhagen, Denmark
Tel: +45 30 20 02 33
Fax: +45 30 20 02 56
design@uniqueinterieur.dk
www.uniqueinterieur.com

WWW.ELECTRIC-SWITCHES.COM
*An electric switches directory
including rotary, pushbutton, rocker,
toggle, snap action, slide, and
miniature switches as well as
illuminated switches and marine
switches*

KITCHENS

units & surfaces

FEENY
*Kitchen and bathroom storage,
shelving, speciality fittings*
Knape & Vogt Manufacturing Co
270 Oak Industrial Drive NE
Grand Rapids MI 49505
Tel: 616-459-3311
Fax: 616-459-3467
postmstr@kv.com
www.kv.com

FORMICA CORPORATION
10155 Reading Road
Cincinnati OH 45241
Tel: 513-786-3400
Fax: 513-786-3024
www.formica.com

IKEA
*Furnishing store selling kitchen units
and furniture*
(See Storage)

STONE PANELS
*Supplier of Pietro Taro limestone,
Azul Macauba Brazilian granite,
and Carrara marble*
1725 Sandy Lake Road
Carrollton TX 75006
Tel: 972-446-1776 or 800-328-6275
Fax: 972-245-3749 or 800-752-0783
www.stonepanels.com

TILE MOSAICS.COM
Supplier of mosaic tiles
8133 Firestone Boulevard
Downey CA 90241
Tel: 562-904-8446
Fax: 562-622-7123
www.tilemosaics.com

plumbing

THG USA
6601 Lyons Road, Suite C-10
Coconut Creek FL 33073
Tel: 954-425-8225
Fax: 954-425-8301
www.thgusa.com

BARBER WILSONS & CO LTD
*Kitchen and laboratory taps
and bathroom and shower
fittings, including models similar
to that p149tr*
Tel: +44 20 8888 3461
Fax: +44 20 8888 2041
sales@barwil.co.uk
www.barwil.co.uk
US Distributor:
Soho Corp
Tel: 631-287-2700

BRASS & TRADITIONAL SINKS
Export internationally
Tel: +44 1291 650743
Fax: +44 1291 650827
info@sinks.co.uk
www.sinks.co.uk.

BRISTAN LTD
*Kitchen and bathroom taps, shower
fittings, and bathroom accessories
International exports*
Tel: +44 1827 68525
Fax: +44 1827 68553
orders@bristan.com
www.bristan.com

CARRON PHOENIX LTD
*Kitchen sinks in stainless steel,
ceramic, and reconstituted quartz,
also taps, including the Pinto model,
similar to p147t*
North American distributor:
Kindred Industries
P.O. Box 190
1000 Kindred Road
Midland
Ontario L4R 4K9
Tel: 705-526-5427
Fax: 705-526-8055

DORNBRACHT
*Kitchen and bathroom taps and
bathroom accessories*
Armaturenfabrik
Kobbingser Muhle 6
D-58640 Iserlohn, Germany
Tel: +49 2371 4330
Fax: +49 2371 433135
mail@dornbracht.de
Dornbracht USA, Inc.
1700 Executive Drive S Ste 600
Duluth, GA 30096

Tel: 800-774-1181
Fax: 800-899-8527
mail@dornbracht.com
www.dornbracht.com

FRANKE KITCHEN SYSTEMS
*Sinks in stainless steel, ceramic, and
high-spec composites; taps, work-
centre accessories, and water
purification systems*
3050 Campus Drive, Suite 500
Hatfield PA 19440
Tel: 215-822-6590
Fax: 215-822-5873
www.franke.com

GEMINI BATH & KITCHEN
PRODUCTS
1501 East Broadway Boulevard
Tuscon, AZ 85719
Tel: 520-770-0667
Fax: 520-770-9964
www.geminibkp.com

GROHE GMBH
*Kitchen and bathroom taps and
showers*
Postfach 1353
32457 Porta Westfalica, Germany
Tel: +49 18 02/66 00 00
www.grohe.com
Grohe America, Inc.
241 Covington Drive
Bloomingdale IL 60108
Tel: 630-582-7711
FAX: 630-582-7722
info@GroheAmerica.com
Grohe Canada, Inc.
1226 Lakeshore Road East
Mississauga, Ontario
Canada L5E 1F9
Phone: 905-271-2929
Fax: 905-271-9494
info@GroheCanada.com
www.GROHEAmerica.com

HANSGROHE GMBH
*Axor, Pharo, and Hansgrohe taps;
also whirlpool bathtubs, airbaths,
and showers*
Auestr. 5–9
77761 Schiltach, Germany
Tel: +49 7836-51-0
Fax: +49 7836-51-1300
www.hansgrohe.com
Hansgrohe USA
Tel: 800-334-0455.
www.hansgrohe-usa.com

HARRINGTON BRASSWORKS
7 Pearl Court
Allendale NJ 07401
Tel: 201-818-1300
Fax: 201-818-0099
hwb@harringtonbrassworks.com

HERBEAU CREATIONS OF AMERICA
*Period-style taps, brass and ceramic
sinks, and bathroom fittings*
2795 Davis Blvd., #E
Naples FL 34104
Tel: 941-417-5368
Fax: 800-547-0084
herbeau@earthlink.net
www.herbeau.com

LEFROY BROOKS
*Faucets, including Liberty Bibcocks,
similar to the bib faucets page 146ac*
Tel +44 1992 448 300
Fax +44 1992 448 301
info@lefroybrooks.co.uk
Lefroy Brooks USA
10 Leonard Street, Suite 2N
New York NY 10013
Tel: 212-226-2242
Fax: 212-226-3003
info@lefroybrooks.co.uk
www.lefroybrooks.com

QUINTESSENTIALS
*Stock faucets by Harrington
Brassworks and Gemini*
532 Amsterdam Avenue
New York, NY 10024
Tel: 212-877-1919 or 888-676-BATH
Fax: 212-721-6172
www.qkb.com

PHYLRICH INTERNATIONAL
*Faucets similar to that featured
p146bcl*
1000 North Orange Drive
Los Angeles CA 90038-2318
Tel: 323-467-3143 or 800-421-3190
Fax: 323-871-8021
www.phylrich.com

SAMUEL HEATH AND SONS PLC
*Taps, showers, bathroom
accessories, architectural hardware*
Tel: +44 121 772 2303
Fax: +44 121 772 3334
info@samuel-heath.com
www.samuel-heath.com

T & S BRASS AND BRONZE WORKS
INC.
Tel: 800-476-4103
Fax: 800-868-0084
www.tsbrass.com

TONI ARMATUR
www.toni.dk

VOLA
*Range of Arne Jacobsen
designed taps*
Lunavej 2
DK-8700 Horsens, Denmark
Tel: +45 7023 5500
Fax: +45 7023 5511
sales@vola.dk
www.vola.dk
US Distributor:
Hastings Tile and IL Bagno Collection
30 Commercial Street
Freeport NY 11520
Tel: 516-379-3500 or 800-351-0038
Fax: 516-379-3187
vola@hastings30.com
www.hastingstilebath.com
www.vola.com

appliances

AGA RANGES
Tel: 800-633-9200
www.aga-ranges.com

AMANA APPLIANCES
2800 220th Trail
Amana IA 52204
Tel: 800-843-0304
www.amana.com

BOFFI
Kitchens and appliances
Via Oberdan 70
20030 Lentate s/S(Mi), Italy
Tel: +39 0362 5341
Fax: +39 0362 565077

BOSCH
BSH Home Appliances Corporation
5551 McFadden Avenue
Huntington Beach CA 92649
Tel: 800-866-2022
www.boschappliances.com

BRITANNIA
The Range Cooker Co. plc.
Tel: +44 1253 471111
Fax: +44 1253 471136
enquiry@rangecooker.co.uk
www.rangecooker.co.uk

FISHER & PAYKEL APPLIANCES INC.
*Laundry, refrigeration, dishwashing,
cooking appliances*
27 Hubble
Irvine CA 92618
Tel: 800-863-5394
Fax: 949-790-8911
www.usa.fisherpaykel.com

FRIGIDAIRE
*Cookers, dishwashers, freezers,
refrigerators, and laundry appliances*
Electrolux International
3 Parkway Center
Pittsburgh PA 15220
Tel: 412 928 8100
www.frigidaire.com

GAGGENAU HAUS GERATE GMBH
Domestic appliances
Postfach 1201
D-76552 Gaggenau
Baden
Germany
Tel: +49 7225-78026
Fax: +49 7225-967190
www.gaggenau.com

GE (GENERAL ELECTRIC)
*Refrigerators and freezers, washers
and dryers, dishwashers,
compactors, cookers*
Tel: 800-626-2000
www.geappliances.com

KITCHENAID
Counter-top and major appliances
1701 KitchenAid Way
Greenville OH 45331
USA
Tel: 800-541-6390
Fax: 800-422-1230
www.kitchenaid.com

LIEBHERR-AMERICA, INC.
4100 Chestnut Ave.
P.O. Box Drawer O.
Newport News VA 23605
Tel: 757-245-5251
www.liebherr-us.com

MIELE, INC.
www.miele.de
9 Independence Way
Princeton, NJ 08540
Tel: 609-419-9898 or 800-843-7231
www.miele.com

SMEG
*Italian manufacturers of domestic
appliances*
www.smeg.it
North American Distributor:
Integrated Appliances
1290 Martin Grove Road
Toronto, ON
M9W 4X3 CANADA
Tel: 416-646-2500
Fax 416-646-2505
intappltd@aol.com

VIKING RANGE CORPORATION
*Professional range cookers,
refrigeration, ovens, and dishwashers*
111 Front Street
Greenwood
Mississippi 38930
Tel. 866-451-4133.or 888-VIKING1
www.vikingrange.com

WOLF APPLIANCES CO. LLC,
Sub-Zero refrigeration
P.O. Box 44848
Madison WI 53744
Tel: 800-222-7820
Fax: 608-271-2233
www.subzero.com.

ZANUSSI
Part of Electrolux Group
18013 Cleveland Parkway, Suite 100
Cleveland OH 44135-0920
Tel: 216-898-1800
Fax: 216-898-2366
www.na.electrolux.com

BATHROOMS

miscellaneous

*To find a bathroom remodeling
contractor in your area:*
www.pricequotes.com/homeimprove
ment/bathroom.html

LINEABETA
Bathroom accessories
Strada Statale 11
KM331-36053 Gambellara V1
Italy
Tel: +39 444 644 644
Fax: +39 444 644 600
www.lineabeta.com

fittings & fixtures

AGAPE SRL
Via Po Barna 69
46031 Corregio Micheli di Bagnolo
San Vito (MN), Italy
Tel: +39 0376 250311
Fax: +39 0376 250330
info@agapedesign.it
www.agapedesign.it

ALTERNATIVE PLANS
*Stockists of contemporary Italian
Agape bathrooms and Boffi kitchens*
Tel: +44 20 7228 6460
Fax: +44 20 7924 1164
altplans@circon.co.uk
www.alternative-plans.co.uk

BARBER WILSONS & CO
Traditional taps and shower fittings
(See Kitchens)

B.C. SANITAN
Traditional-style bathroom fittings
(See Jacuzzi)

BISQUE
Designer radiators
244 Belsize Road
London NW6 4BT, UK
Tel: +44 20 7328 2225
Fax: +44 20 7328 9845
mail@bisque.co.uk
www.bisque.co.uk
Available in US through:
3-D Laboratory
268 Water Street
New York NY10038
Tel: 212-791-7070
info@3-Dcon.com
www.3-dlaborartory.com

BOWDEN HOMES
*Bathtubs, glass windows, and
custom built-ins*
138 Timber Creek
Cordova TN 38018
Tel: 901-758-6200 or 877-4-BOWDEN
info@bowdenhomes.com
www.bowdenhomes.com

CLAWFOOT SUPPLY
*Complete supply of authentic
reproduction clawfoot tubs (feet in
chrome or brass), pedestal and
console sinks, Topaz copper soaking
tubs, polished nickel fixtures,
handmade copper sinks, shower
heads, and more*
957 Western Avenue
Covington, KY 41011
Tel: 877-682-4192
www.clawfootsupply.com

COLOURWASH
*Well-edited selection of
contemporary bathroom fittings
and accessories*
165 Chamberlayne Road
London NW10 3NU, UK
Tel: +44 20 8459 8918
Fax: +44 20 8459 4280
sales@colourwash.co.uk
www.colourwash.co.uk

C.P. HART
*Bathroom ceramics, furniture, taps,
bathtubs, showers, and accessories*
Newnham Terrace
Hercules Road
London SE1 7DR, UK
Tel: +44 20 7902 1000
Fax: +44 20 7902 1001
www.cphart.co.uk

DORNBRACHT
(See Kitchens)

DÜKER SANITÄR GMBH
Am Wendelsberg 24
97289 Thüngen, Germany
Tel: + 49 9360/90620
Fax: +49 9360/906239
info@dueker-sanitaer.de
www.dueker-sanitaer.de

DURAVIT AG
Designers Philippe Starck, Dieter
Sieger, and Phoenix Product Design
(composed of the German duo Tom
Schonherr and Andreas Haug)
emphasize purity of line, clarity of
form, and excellence in workmanship
Werderstrasse 36
D-7832 Hornberg, Germany
Tel: +49 78 33 70 0
Fax: +49 78 33 70 289
info@duravit.de
Duravit
1750 Breckinridge Parkway, Suite 500
Duluth, GA 30096
Tel: 770-931-3575 or 888-DURAVIT
Fax: 770-931-8454
www.duravit.com

GROHE
Traditional and contemporary faucets
and showers
(See Kitchens)

HANSGROHE
Showerheads and faucets in
contemporary designs
(See Kitchens)

HIGH TECH
Contemporary washbasins, including
Pollux series
www.hightech-vola-usa.com

INFORM
(See Lighting)

JACUZZI WHIRLPOOL BATH
Sanitaryware, showers, brassware,
whirlpool bathtubs, and accessories
2121 N. California Blvd., Suite 475
Walnut Creek CA 94596
Tel: 925-938-7411
Fax: 925-938-3025
www.jacuzzi.com

KALLISTA
Luxury bathroom products designed
by Barbara Berry and Michael S.
Smith; mahogany tub surrounds,
sleek and modern fixtures
444 Highland Drive
Mailstop 032

Kohler WI 53044
Tel: 888-4-KALLISTA
www.kallistainc.com

KOHLER
Many bathtub, sink, and bathroom
designs and accessories; locations
throughout U.S.
444 Highland Drive
Kohler WI 53044
Tel: 920-457-4441 or 800-456-4537
www.kohler.com

ORION HARDWARE
Sleek curvilinear bathroom fixtures,
taps, and controls designed by Carlo
Bartoli, Castiglia Associati, Columbo
Design, Makio Hasuike, and more
80 Marycroft Avenue, Unit 2
Woodbridge, Ontario
Canada L4L 5Y5
Tel: 800-226-6627
Fax: 905-850-2916
www.orionhardware.com

PERRIN & ROWE
Country faucets similar to that
featured p167c
SN Delia Architectural & Decorative
Hardware
53795 Route 25
Southold NY 11971
Tel: 631-765-5015 or 866-765-5015
Fax: 631-765-5016
www.sndelia.com

PORCHER™ BRAND OF AMERICAN
STANDARD
Wall-mounted basins
P.O. Box 6820
1 Centennial Plaza
Piscataway NJ 08855-6820
Tel: 800-359-3261
www.americanstandard-us.com

SAMUEL HEATH & SONS PLC
Taps, showers, bathroom
accessories, architectural hardware
(See Kitchens)

SANTRIC LTD
Stainless-steel lavatories, industrial
sinks, and basins
Downley Road
Havant PO9 2YD, UK
Tel: +44 23 9248 8755
Fax: +44 23 9248 8766
info@santric.co.uk
www.santric.co.uk

SOTTINI
Bathroom fittings and taps
The Bathroom Works
National Avenue

Kingston upon Hull HU5 4HS, UK
Tel: +44 1482 449513
Fax: + 44 1482 445886
www.sottini.co.uk

TAKAGI INDUSTRIAL CO. USA Inc.
Japanese bathtub designs
6 Goddard
Irvine, CA 92618
Tel: 949-453-8388
Fax: 949-453-8498
E-mail: takagi@takagi-usa.com
www.takagi-usa.com

VINTAGE PLUMBING
Original and restored to perfection
bathroom antiques by all the great
old manufacturing companies; also
have toilets similar to that featured
p164a
9645 Sylvia Avenue
Northridge, CA 91324
Tel: 818-772-1721
www.vintageplumbing.com

VOLA
(See Kitchens)

WATERWORKS
Exquisite collection of bathroom
fixtures, furniture, lighting, and
fittings
23 West Putnam Avenue
Greenwich CT 06830
Tel: 800-998-BATH or 203-869-7766
www.waterworks.com

WHIRLPOOLBATH STORE
Soaking tubs, shower accessories,
toilets, showers, bidets and bidet
faucets
P.O. Box 429
Middletown NY 10940
Tel: 877-613-8139
Fax: 845-343-1617
info@whirlpoolbathstore.com
www.whirlpoolbathstore.com

WONDER SHOWER HEAD
A great variety of shower-head
designs, in brushed-nickel, brass,
copper, platinum, and chrome, in
sloping, extension, or dual-arm
designs
Tel: 800-595-0385
bret@showeringgifts.com
www.showeringgifts.com

surface finishes
FIRED EARTH
Wall and floor tiles and bathroom
fittings
(See Flooring)

GAM-ROBERT CERAMIC TILE INC.
Represents and sells ceramic tiles
and marble from manufacturers
in Spain, Italy, Greece, India, Brazil,
and Portugal
8181 NW 36th Street, Suite 1901
Miami FL 33166
Tel: 305-639-9874
Fax: 305-463-9223
www.gam-robert.com

HARVEY MARIA
Cork tiles printed with photographic
images
Tel: +44 20 8516 7788
Fax: +44 20 8516 7789
www.harveymaria.co.uk

LITHOFIN
German range of sealing, cleaning
and protection products
www.lithofin.de

LONGMEAD CERAMICS
Ceramic tiles including tiles with
integral bathroom accessories
Millway Industrial Estate
Axminster EX3 5HU, UK
Tel: +44 1297 33578

MAJESTIC SHOWER COMPANY LTD
Shower doors, enclosures, and
bath screens
Tel: +44 1279 443644
Fax: +44 1279 635074
info@majesticshowers.com
www.majesticshowers.com

PARIS EQUIPMENT
MANUFACTURING
Custom designers in metal
fabrication, powder coating, polymer
coating, and plastisol dipping
21 Scott Avenue
P.O. Box 70
Paris, Ontario
Canada N3L 3E5
Tel: 519-442-3324
Fax: 519-442-0111
www.peml.com

PERSPEX
Perspex, Prismex and Lucite acrylic
sheet; a list of fabricators can be
found on the websites
Tel: +44 1254 874000
www.perspex.co.uk
www.lucite.com

RIDOUT PLASTICS
Plastic shower screens as featured
p160
5535 Ruffin Road
San Diego, CA 92123

Tel: 800-4-RIDOUT or 858-560-1551
Fax: 858-560-1941
www.ridoutplastics.com

TIKKURILA COATINGS LTD
Speacialist coatings including
chlorinated rubber paint for
swimming pools
Tel: +44 161 764 6017
info@tikkurila.co.uk
www.tikkurila-coatings.co.uk

YOUNG BLOCK
Glass blocks in a variety of shapes
and styles
2200 West Gardner Lane
Tucson AZ 85705
Tel: 520-887-1234
Fax: 520-888-2079
www.youngblock.com

ARCHITECTS AND DESIGNERS WHOSE WORK IS FEATURED IN THIS BOOK

JONATHAN ADLER
465 Broome Street
New York NY 10013
Tel: 212 941 8950
Pottery lighting and textiles
Page 102b.

ANDERSON ARCHITECTS
555 West 25th Street
New York NY 10001
Tel: 212 620 0996
Fax: 212 620 5299
info@andersonarch.com
www.andersonarch.com
Page 67bl.

NICHOLAS ARBUTHNOTT
Arbuthnott Ladenbury Architects
Architects & Urban Designers
15 Gosditch Street
Cirencester GL7 2AG
and
VANESSA ARBUTHNOTT FABRICS
The Tallet
Calmsden
Cirencester GL7 5ET
www.vanessaarbuthnott.co.uk
and
COUNTRY HOUSE WALKS LTD
Self-catering accommodation/ weekend breaks
The Tallet
Calmsden
Cirencester GL7 5ET
www.thetallet.co.uk
Pages 15r, 154al.

ASFOUR GUZY
594 Broadway, Suite 1204
New York NY 10012
Tel: 212 334 9350
Fax: 212 334 9009
Page 122br.

ASH SAKULA ARCHITECTS
24 Rosebery Avenue
London EC1R 4SX, UK
Tel: +44 20 7837 9735
Fax: +44 20 7837 9708
robert@ashsak.com
www.ashsak.com
Pages 55br, 129br,146al, 149br, 154ac, 155ac.

AZMAN OWENS
Architects
8 St Albans place
London NW1 0NX, UK
Tel: +44 20 7354 2955
Fax: +44 20 7354 2966
Pages 50al, 158al.

BABYLON DESIGN LTD
Lighting Designers
301 Fulham Road
London SW10 9QH, UK
Tel: +44 20 7376 7233
info@babylondesign.demon.co.uk
Lights by up-and-coming designers such as Peter Wylly, Ross Menuez and Roland Simmons
Page 132a.

JOHN BARMAN INC.
Interior design & decoration
500 Park Avenue
New York NY 10022
Tel: 212 838 9443
john@barman.com
www.johnbarman.com
Pages 8a, 19al, 136, 145bl, 150a, 150bl, 150bc, 152a, 157al, 165ar.

BATAILLE & iBENS
Claire Bataille & Paul ibens
Design NV
Architects
Vekestratt 13 Bus 14
2000 Antwerpen
Belgium
Tel: +32 3 231 3593
Fax: +32 3 213 8639
Pages 57r, 60bl, 86ar, 86br, 99a, 106br, 172bc.

CHARLES BATESON DESIGN CONSULTANTS
Interior Design
18 Kings Road, St Margaret's
Twickenham TW1 2QS, UK
Tel: +44 20 8892 3141
Fax: +44 20 8891 6483
Charles.bateson@btinternet.com
Pages 3c, 3r, 6ac, 9br, 19bl, 21c, 29br, 36ar, 55ar, 90, 100ar, 108a, 142bc, 158br, 166ac, 168ar.

BEDMAR & SHI DESIGNERS PTE LTD
A Singapore based firm established in 1980 specializing in residential projects and also in interior design mainly for restaurants and offices
12a Keong Saik Road
Singapore 089119
Tel: +65 22 77117
Fax: +65 22 77695
Front jacket

ROBERTO BERGERO
Interior Designer
4 rue St. Gilles
75003 Paris
France
Tel: +33 1 42 72 03 51

robertobergero@club-internet.fr
Page 70b.

BILHUBER INC
330 East 59th Street, 6th Floor
New York NY 10022
Tel: 212 308 4888
Pages 73al, 103ar.

STEPHEN BLATT ARCHITECTS
Architectural Design Firm
10, Danforth Street
Portland, Maine 04101
Tel: 207 761 5911
Fax: 207 761 2105
sba@sbarchitects.com
Page 103al.

L.B.D.A.
Laura Bohn Design Associates, Inc.
30 West 26th Street
New York NY 10010
Tel: 212 645 3636
Fax: 212 645 3639
Pages 120cr, 122bl.

FELIX BONNIER
7 rue St Claude
75003 Paris
France
Tel: +33 42 26 09 83
Pages 36al, 146bl.

BOWLES & LINARES
32 Hereford Road
London W2 5AJ, UK
Tel: +44 20 7229 9886
Pages 9bl, 20al, 139cr.

BRIFFA PHILIPS
19–21 Holywell Hill
St Albans
Herts AL1 1EZ, UK
Tel: +44 1727 840567
Page 64bl.

MARK BROOK DESIGN
7 Sunderland Terrace
London W2 5PA, UK
Tel: +44 20 7221 8106
Pages 153bl, 154ar.

BROOKES STACEY RANDALL
New Hibernia House
Winchester Walk
London SE1 9AG, UK
Tel: +44 20 7403 0707
Fax: +44 20 7403 0880
info@bsr-architects.com
Pages 9bc, 30c, 31, 58–59, 100al, 162ac.

HUGH BROUGHTON ARCHITECTS
Award winning architects
4 Addison Bridge Place

London W14 8XP, UK
Tel: +44 20 7602 8840
Fax: +44 20 7602 5254
hugh@hbarchitects.demon.co.uk
Pages 2bl, 50ar, 137br, 145al.

CABOT DESIGN LTD
Interior Design
1925 Seventh Avenue, Suite 71
New York NY10026
Tel: 212 222 9488
eocabot@aol.com
Page 97

CARDEN CUNIETTI
83 Westbourne Park Road
London W2 5QH, UK
Tel: +44 20 7229 8559
Fax: +44 20 7229 8799
www.carden-cunietti.com
Pages 168br, 169br.

GARTH CARTER
Specialist interiors painter
Tel: +44 958 412953
Page 164l.

CIRCUS ARCHITECTS
Unit 1, Summer Street
London EC1R 5BD, UK
Tel: +44 20 7833 1999
Pages 50b, 53bl, 57l, 60al, 60cl, 61ar, 64br, 65, 78l, 119a, 122al, 129ar, 152bl.

DAVID COLLINS
Architecture & Design
Unit 6 & 7
Chelsea Wharf
Lots Road
London SW10 0QJ, UK
Tel: +44 20 7349 5900
Page 20br.

SIMON CONDER ASSOCIATES
Architects & Designers
Nile Street Studios
8 Nile street
London N1 7RF, UK
Tel: +44 20 7251 2144
Fax: +44 20 7251 2145
e.simon@simonconder.co.uk
Pages 161bl, 164r.

DLB CORDIER
Church Farm Oast Conversion by DLB
Cordier – *Architect*
danielcordier@compuserve.com
Pages 67al, 85cr, 99b.

DAD ASSOCIATES
112–6 Old Street
London EC1V 9BD, UK
Tel: +44 20 7336 6488
Pages 42b, 172c.

JOËLLE DARBY
Architect
Darby Maclellan Partnership
Unit 3 Limehouse Cut
46 Morris Road
London E14 6NQ, UK
Tel: +44 20 7987 4432
darby.maclellan@tinyonline.co.uk
Page 160cl.

SANDY DAVIDSON DESIGN
1505 Viewsite Terrace
Los Angeles, CA 90069
Fax: 320 659 2107
SandSandD@aol.com
Pages 26a, 78r, 161a.

DOLS WONG ARCHITECTS
Architects specialising in private residences, one-off shops and restaurants.
Loft 3, 329 Harrow Road
London W9 3RB, UK
Tel: +44 20 7266 2129
Fax: +44 20 7266 2179
dolswong@btinternet.com
Pages 1, 2cr, 6br, 19br, 91al, 111br, 113br, 120ac, 120br, 121.

ROBERT DYE ASSOCIATES
68–74 Rochester Place
London NW1 9JX
Page 42ar.

EGER ARCHITECTS
Architects & Landscape Architects
2 D'eynsford Road
London SE5 7EB, UK
Tel: +44 20 7701 6771
Fax: +44 20 7708 5716
design@egerarchitects.com
www.egerarchitects.com
Pages 5, 9ar, 11al, 19ac, 19ar, 20c, 24al, 28al, 28ac, 30ar, 45al, 98b, 122bc.

EMERY & CIE AND NOIR D'IVORIE
Rue de L'Hôpital 25–29
Brussels
Belgium
Tel: +32 2 513 5892
Fax: +32 5 513 3970
Pages 33r, 39ar.

FAT
Appletree Cottage
116–120 Golden Lane
London EC1Y 0TL, UK
Tel: +44 20 7251 6735
Fax: +44 20 7251 6730
fat@fat.co.uk
www.fat.co.uk
Page 15c.

FILER & COX
Architectural Deviants
194 Bermondsey Street
London SE1 3TQ, UK
Tel: +44 20 7357 7574
Fax: +44 20 7357 7573
iru@filerandcox.com
www.filerandcox.com
Pages 7c, 20cl, 44, 72al, 72bl,
73bl, 142cr, 154bl, 157ac, 162br,
170b, 172bl.

GABELLINI ASSOCIATES
*Michael Gabellini AIA, Principal
designer. Dan Garbowit AIA,
Managing Principal Ralph Bellandi.
Sal Tranchina, Jonathan Knowles
AIA, Project Architects. Stephanie
Kim, Lisa Monteleone, Tom
Vandenbout, Project Team*
665 Broadway, Suite 706
New York NY 10012
Tel: 212 388 1700
Fax: 212 388 1808
Page 61c.

ZINA GLAZEBROOK
ZG Design
10 Wireless Road
East Hampton NY 11937
Tel: 631 329 7486
Fax: 631 329 2087
dzina@ATT.net
www.zgdesign.com
Pages 34–35.

GLOSS LTD
Designers of home accessories
274 Portobello Road
London W10 5TE, UK
Tel: +44 20 8960 4146
Fax: +44 20 8960 4842
pascale@glossltd.u-net.com
Pages 96–97

CHRISTOPHE GOLLUT
Alistair Colvin Limited
116 Fulham Road
London SW3 6HU
Pages 38–39, 39b.

JAMES GORST ARCHITECTS
35 Lambs Conduit Street
London WC1N 3NG, UK
Tel: +44 20 7831 8300
Pages 66a, 66cr, 91ar, 158bl.

HESTER GRAY
25 Pembridge Villas
London W11 3EP, UK
Tel: +44 20 7229 3162
Page 155b.

MARK GUARD ARCHITECTS
161 Whitfield Street
London W1P 5RY, UK
Tel: +44 20 7380 1199
Pages 29ar, 43a.

WILLIAM R. HEFNER AIA
William Hefner Architect L.L.C
5820 Wilshire Boulevard, Suite 601
Los Angeles CA 90036
Tel: 323 931 1365
Fax: 323 931 1368
wh@williamhefner.com
www.williamhefner.com
Pages 26a, 78r, 161a.

ALASTAIR HENDY
*Food writer, art director and
designer*
Fax: +44 20 7739 6040
Pages 58, 101b, 169ac.

GUY HILLS
Photographer
Tel/fax: +44 20 7916 2610
guyhills@hotmail.com
Pages 7a, 22, 28ar, 35c&bl, 59, 81r,
98ac.

HIRST PACIFIC LTD
250 Lafayette Street
New York NY 10012
Tel: 212 625 3670
Fax: 212 625 3673
hirstpacific@earthlink.net
Pages 62–63, 139c.

HM2 ARCHITECTS
*Architects & Designers
Richard Webb, Project Director
Andrew Hanson, Director*
33–37 Charterhouse Square
London EC1M 6EA, UK
Tel: +44 20 7600 5151
Fax: +44 20 7600 1092
andrew.hanson@harper-mackay.co.uk
Pages 17, 166cl.

PHILIP HOOPER
Interior Designer
Studio 30, The Old Latchmere School
38 Burns Road
London SW11 5GY, UK
Tel: +44 20 7978 6662
Fax: +44 20 7223 3713
Page 103bl.

JOHN C HOPE
Architects
3 St. Bernard's Crescent
Edinburgh EH4 1NR, UK
Tel: +44 131 315 2215
Fax: +44 131 315 2911
Pages 25b, 42al, 85br.

**HUDSON FEATHERSTONE
ARCHITECTS**
49–59 Old Street
London EC1V 9HX, UK
Tel: +44 20 7490 5656
Pages 34c, 45b, 53al, 82a, 87.

HUT SACHS STUDIO
Architecture & Interior Design
414 Broadway
New York NY 10013
Tel: 212 219 1567
Fax: 212 219 1677
hutsachs@hutsachs.com
www.hutsachs.com
Page 142a.

INTERNI PTY LTD
Interior Design Consultancy
15–19 Boundary Street
Rushcutter's Bay
Sydney 2010
Australia
Pages 7b, 12, 39br.

MALIN IOVINO DESIGN
Tel: +44 20 7252 3542
Fax: +44 20 7252 3542
iovino@btinternet.com
Pages 125ar, 125ac.

IPL INTERIORS
Thames House, Unit 26Cl
140 Battersea Park Road
London SW11 4NY, UK
Tel: +44 20 7622 3009
Fax: +44 20 7622 2246
ipl.interiors@virgin.net
Pages 14bc, 38bl, 71 all above, 89al,
91br, 95, 100h, 108bl, 111a both,
111cl, 117r, 118al, 123bl, 126al,
135ar, 135bc.

GAVIN JACKSON
Tel: +44 7050 097561
Page 139bl.

JOANNA JEFFERSON ARCHITECTS
222 Oving Road
Chichester PO19 4EJ, UK
Tel: +44 1243 532398
Fax: +44 1243 531 550
jjeffearch@aol.com
Page 67br.

JOHNSON NAYLOR
13 Britton Street
London EC1M 5SX, UK
Tel: +44 20 7490 8885
Fax: +44 20 7490 0038
brian.johnson@johnsonnaylor.co.uk
Pages 56, 66cl, 172ac.

JUAN PECK FOON
*Resources + Planning Design
Consultants*
73 Cardiff Grove
Singapore 558939
Tel: +65 382 4518
Fax: +65 382 4865
peckfoon@singnet.com.sg
Page 30bl.

JUST DESIGN LTD
80 Fifth Avenue, 18th Floor
New York NY 10011
Tel: 212 243 6544
Fax: 212 229 1112
wbp@angel.net
Page 13.

ANGELA KEARSEY DESIGNS
*General interior design and
decoration—wall/floor coverings,
curtains, fabrics and accessories*
Tel: +44 20 7483 0967
Fax: +44 20 7483 1629
Angela.Kearsey@btinternet.com
Pages 1, 2cr, 6br, 19br, 91al, 111br,
113br, 120ac, 120br, 121.

SEAN KELLY GALLERY
520 West 29th Street
New York NY 10001
Tel: 212 239 1181
Fax: 212 239 2467
www.skny.com
Pages 14bl, 113al, 141bl.

ANGELA KENT
Architect
Kenström Design Pty Ltd
92 Cathedral Street
Woolloomooloo NSW 2011
Australia
Page 139bl.

STEVEN LEARNER STUDIO
Architecture and interior design
307 Seventh Avenue
New York NY 10001
Tel: 212 741 8583
Fax: 212 741 2180
info@stevenlearnerstudio.com
www.stevenlearnerstudio.com
Pages 14bl, 113al, 141bl.

KAYODE LIPEDE
Tel: +44 20 7794 7535
Page 152bl.

DALE LOTH ARCHITECTS
1 Cliff Road
London NW1 9AJ, UK
Tel: +44 20 7485 4003
Fax: +44 20 7284 4490
mail@dalelotharchitects.ltd.uk
Pages 165bl, 165bc, 169cr.

RANDALL L. MAKINSON
RLM Associates
Restoration Consultants
Fax: 626 449 2059
makinson@earthlink.net
Page 120cl.

NICOLETTA MARAZZA
Via G Morone, 8
20121 Milan
Italy
Tel/fax: +39 2 7601 4482
Pages 105bl, 115al.

MARINO + GIOLITO
161 West 16th Street
New York NY 10011
Tel/fax: 212 675 5737
Pages 113ar, 166al, 170c.

**MARMOL & RADZINER +
ASSOCIATES, ARCHITECTURE +
CONSTRUCTION**
2902, Nebraska Avenue
Santa Monica CA 90404
Tel: 310 264 1814
Fax: 310 264 1817
www.marmol-radziner.com
Pages 26–27a, 81l.

PAUL MATHIEU
Interior Design
France:
12 rue Matheron
13100 Aix-en-Provence
France
Tel: +33 4 42 23 97 77
Fax: +33 4 42 23 97 59
USA:
7 East 14th Street, # 805
New York NY 10003
Tel: 646 638 4031
Page 171al.

MCDOWELL + BENEDETTI
62 Rosebury Avenue
London EC1R 4RR, UK
Tel: +44 20 7278 8810
Pages 37a, 41a.

DAVID MELLOR DESIGN
*David Mellor cutlery is manufactured
in the Round Building; the Country
Shop sells cutlery, kitchenware,
tableware and British craftware*
The Round Building & Country Shop
Hathersage
Sheffield S32 1BA, UK
Tel: +44 1433 650220
Fax: +44 1433 650944
davidmellor@UKOnline.co.uk
Page 62r.

JEAN-LOUIS MÉNARD
32 Boulevard de l'Hopital
75005 Paris
France
Tel: +33 43 36 31 74
Page 165al.

FRÉDÉRIC MÉRCHICHE
4 rue de Thorigny
75003 Paris
France
Pages 33bl, 45ac.

DAVID MIKHAIL ARCHITECTS
68/74 Rochester Place
London NW1 9JX, UK
Tel: +44 20 7485 4696
Fax: +44 20 7267 8661
www.dmikhail.freeserve.co.uk
Pages 165br, 170al.

MONEO BROCK STUDIO
371 Broadway
New York NY 10013
USA
Tel: 212 625 0308
Fax: 212 625 0309
www.moneobrock.com
Pages 2al, 6al, 18al, 18r, 88, 93ar,
140cr, 142a, 147a, 151al, 151ac,
153cl, 154–155b 155c, 160a, 167a.

MOOArc
Architects
198 Blackstock Road
London N5 1EN, UK
Tel: +44 20 7354 1729
Fax: +44 20 7354 1730
studio@mooarc.com
www.mooarc.com
Pages 29al, 86l, 91bc.

**MOORE RUBLE YUDELL
ARCHITECTS & PLANNERS.**
933 Pico Boulevard
Santa Monica CA 90405
Tel: 310 450 1400
Fax: 310 450 1403
Pages 11bl, 24c.

MULLMAN SEIDMAN ARCHITECTS
Architecture & interior design
443 Greenwich Street, # 2A
New York NY 10013
Tel: 212 431 0770
Fax: 212 431 8428
msa@mullmanseidman.com
dmullman@mullmanseidman.com
pseidman@mullmanseidman.com
www.mullmanseidman.com
Pages 8c, 8b,20ac, 89bl, 98ar, 105al,
106bl, 112, 124r, 127l, 135br, 137ar,
140br, 141al, 143a, 143b, 148r,
152br, 153br, 157b, 171ar, 171b, 173l.

FRANÇOIS MURACCIOLE
Architect
54 rue de Montreuil
75011 Paris
France
Tel: +33 1 43 71 33 03
francois.muracciole@libertysurf.fr
Pages 71c, 117l, 133al.

MUSEUM OF WELSH LIFE
St Fagan's
Cardiff CF5 6XB
Wales
Page 68b.

MICHAEL NATHENSON
Unique Environments
Design & Architecture
33 Florence Street
London N1 2FW, UK
Tel: +44 20 7431 6978
Fax: +44 20 7431 6975
mbn@compuserve.com
www.unique-environments.co.uk
Pages 2ar, 2cl, 19cl, 20al, 20cr, 89c,
89r, 92, 93al, 104, 105br, 108c,
108br, 109, 110a both, 110br, 137al,
137bl, 141r, 149l, 153ar, 162al,
171ac, 172ar.

ROGER OATES DESIGN
Rugs and runners
Shop & Showroom:
1 Munro Terrace
off Cheyne Walk, Chelsea
London SW10 0DL
Studio Shop:
The Long Barn
Eastnor
Ledbury
Herefordshire HR8 1EL, UK
Mail Order Catalogue:
Tel: +44 1531 631611
Pages 53br, 54cr.

OGAWA/DEPARDON ARCHITECTS
137 Varick Street, 4th floor
New York NY 10013
Tel: 212 627 7390
Fax: 212 627 9681
ogawdep@aol.com
Pages 27, 76a, 79.

OREFELT ASSOCIATES
*Design Team: Gunner Orefelt, John
Massey, Gianni Botsford, Jason
Griffiths*
4 Portobello Studios
5 Haydens Place
London W11 1LY, UK
Tel: +44 20 7243 3181
Fax: +44 20 7792 1126
orefelt@msn.com
Pages 9cr, 139al, 156, 161br, 162bl,
170ar.

PARNASSUS
Corso Porta Vittoria, 5
Milan, Italy
Tel: +39 02 78 11 07
Page 147c

CAROLINE PATERSON
50 Lavender Gardens
London SW11 1DD
Page 158ar.

GRAHAM PHILLIPS
Pages 26–27b, 118–119.

CAMPION A PLATT
64l Fifth Avenue
New York NY 10022
Page 35al.

JENNIFER POST DESIGN
Spatial & Interior Designer
25 East 67th Street, 8D
New York NY 10021
Tel: 212 734 7994
Fax: 212 396 2450
jpostdesign@aol.com
Pages 24ac, 49r, 125br.

ALAN POWER ARCHITECTS
5 Haydens Place
London W11 1LY, UK
Tel: +44 20 7229 9375
Fax: +44 20 7221 4172
Pages 75l, 76b, 83.

LENA PROUDLOCK
Denim in Style
Drews House
Leighterton
Gloucestershire GL8 8UN
Tel/fax: +44 1666 890230
Page 148al.

MARK PYNN A.I.A
McMillen Pynn Architecture LLP
PO Box 1068
Sun Valley ID 83353
Tel: 208 622 4656
Fax: 208 726 7108
mpynn@sunvally.net
www.sunvalleyarchitect.com
Pages 14br, 57c, 64al, 67ar.

KARIM RASHID INC.
Industrial design
357 W. 17th Street
New York NY 10011
Tel: 212 929 8657
Fax: 212 929 0247
www.karimrashid.com
Pages 51, 137c, 145ar, 151b.

REED CREATIVE SERVICES LTD
151a Sydney Street
London SW3 6NT, UK

Tel: +44 20 7565 0066
Pages 30al, 119b, 129bc.

NICO RENSCH ARCHITEAM
Tel: +44 411 412 898
Pages 123br, 128, 131a.

RETROUVIUS
Architectural reclaimation and design
Office:
32 York House
Upper Montagu Street
London W1H 1FR, UK
Tel: +44 20 7724 3387
Warehouse/studio:
2A Ravensworth Road
London NW10 5NR, UK
Tel: +44 20 8960 6060
mail@retrouvius.com
www.retrouvious.com
Pages 7a, 22, 28ar, 35l, 59,
81r, 98ac.

RHODE DESIGN
86 Stoke Newington Church Street
London N16 0AP, UK
Tel: +44 20 7275 8261
Pages 21a, 142cl.

JOHANNE RISS
*Stylist, designer, and fashion
designer*
35 Place du Nouveau Marché aux
Graens
1000 Brussels
Belguim
Tel: +32 2 513 0900
Fax: +32 2 514 3284
Page 14al.

DAMIEN ROLAND
Architect
Agence du Centre
6, rue Clovis
45100 Orléans
France
Pages 24ar, 40.

PETER ROMANIUK
The Flower House
Cynthia Street
London N1 9JF, UK
Tel: +44 20 7837 7373
Pages 20bc, 105ar, 110bl, 139bc.

LUIGI ROSSELLI
Surry Hills
2010 Sydney
New South Wales
Australia
Tel: +61 2 9281 1498
Pages 36bl.

EVELYNE ROUSSEL
Tel: +33 1 43 55 76 97
Page 98al.

CHARLES RUTHERFOORD
51 The Chase
London SW4 ONP
Pages 12–13, 41c, 46all above, 52ar,
158cl.

JOSEPHINE RYAN ANTIQUES
63 Abbeville Road
London SW4 9JW, UK
Tel: +44 20 8675 3900
Pages 66b.

**SAGE WIMER COOMBE
ARCHITECTS**
*Project Team: Jennifer Sage, Peter
Coombe, Suzan Selcuk, Peggy Tan*
480 Canal Street Room 1002
New York NY 10013
Tel: 212 226 9600
Page 115ac.

SOPHIE SARIN
Tel: +44 20 7221 4635
Pages 20bl, 146bc.

SCDA ARCHITECTS
10 Teck Lim Road
Singapore 088386
Tel: +65 324 5458
Fax: +65 324 5450
scda@cyberway.com.sg
Pages 15l, 172al.

SCHEFER DESIGN
*David Schefer & Eve-Lynn
Schoenstein*
41 Union Square West, No. 1427
New York NY 10003
Tel: 212 691 9097
Fax: 212 691 9520
scheferdesign@mindspring.com
www.scheferdesign.com
Page 102b.

SHEILA SCHOLES
Designer
Tel: +44 1480 498241
Pages 94a, 155ar.

JOHNSON SCHWINGHAMMER
339 West 38th Street # 9
New York NY 10018
Tel: 212 643 1552
Pages 75br, 77, 85ac, 116, 130bl.

STEVEN SCLAROFF, DESIGNER
801 Greenwich Street
New York NY 10014
Tel: 212 691 7814
Fax: 212 691 7793
sclaroff@aol.com
Pages 151ar, 155al.

MACK SCOGIN MERRILL ELAM ARCHITECTS
Principal architects: Mack Scogin and Merrill Elam
75, J.W. Dobbs Avenue, N.E.
Atlanta, Georgia 30303
Tel: 404 525 6869
Fax: 404 525 7061
Pages 25c, 64ar.

SERGISSION BATES
44 Newman Street
London W1P 3PA, UK
Tel: +44 20 7255 1564
Fax: +44 20 7636 5646
Pages 101ar, 120al.

SHELTON, MINDEL & ASSOCIATES
216 West 18th Street
New York NY 10011
Tel: 212 243 3939
Pages 75br, 77, 85ac, 116, 130bl.

SHEPPARD DAY DESIGN
Tel: +44 20 7821 2002
Pages 23, 91bl, 161bc.

KEN SHUTTLEWORTH
Architect
Page 25a.

SIDNAM PETRONE GARTNER ARCHITECTS
Coty Sidnam, Bill Petrone and Eric Gartner
136 West 21st Street
New York NY 10011
Tel: 212 366 5500
Fax: 212 366 6559
sidnampetr@aol.com
www.spgarchitects.com
Pages 24b, 166c.

STEPHEN SLAN A.I.A
Variations In Architecture Inc.
2156 Hollyridge Drive
Los Angeles CA 90068
Tel: 323 467 4455
Fax: 323 467 6655
Pages 64bc, 68–69, 172br.

NIGEL SMITH
Architect
Tel: +44 20 7278 8802
n-smith@dircon.co.uk
Page 166cr.

SQUARE FOOT PROPERTIES LTD.
50 Britton Street
London EC1M 5UP, UK
Tel: +44 20 7253 2527
Fax: +44 20 7253 2528
Page 85c.

GUY STANSFELD
Tel: +44 20 7727 0133
Pages 111bl, 114.

SETH STEIN ARCHITECT
15 Grand Union Centre
West Row
Ladbrooke Grove
London W10, UK
Tel: +44 20 8968 8581
Pages 60bl, 61bl, 61br, 118bl, 120bl, 123a, 160bl, 162cr, 167b, 167al.

JOHN L. STEWART
SIT, L.L.C.
113–115 Bank Street
New York NY 10014
Tel: 212 620 777
Fax: 212 620 0770
ILSCollection@aol.com
Page 71bl.

STICKLAND COOMBE ARCHITECTURE
258 Lavender Hill
London SW11 1LJ, UK
Tel: +44 20 7924 1699
Fax: +44 20 7652 1788
nick@scadesign.freserve.co.uk
Pages 173c.

SALLY STOREY
John Cullen Lighting
585 King's Road
London SW6 2EH, UK
Tel: +44 20 7371 5400
Page 119b.

TONY SUTTLE
Woods Bagot Pty Ltd
Architects
64 Marine Parade
Southport
Queensland 4215
Australia
Page 16bl.

BRUNO TANQUEREL
Artist
2 Passage St. Sébastien
75011 Paris
France
Tel: +33 1 43 57 03 93
Pages 160bc, 166bc, 166br, 169al.

TAYLOR WOODROW CAPITAL DEVELOPMENTS LTD.
International House
1 St Katherine's Way
London E1 9TW, UK
Tel: +44 20 7488 0555
Page 20br.

TODHUNTER EARLE INTERIORS
Chelsea Reach, 1st floor
79–89 Lots Road
London SW10 0RN, UK
Tel: +44 20 7349 9999
Fax: +44 20 7349 0410
interiors@todhunterearle.com
www.todhunterearle.com
Page 52br.

TOUCH INTERIOR DESIGN
Tel: +44 20 7498 6409
Pages 72ac, 72ar, 96bl.

JIM TRIBE
General Contractor for Orman project
Temple Contracting
20 West 20th Street
New York NY 10011
Pages 8b, 20ac, 89bl, 98ar, 124r, 135r, 140br, 143a, 148r, 171ar, 173l.

TSAO & MCKOWN
Architects
20 Vandam Street, 10th Floor
New York NY 10013
Tel: 212 337 3800
Fax: 212 337 0013
Pages 159l, 163b, 165cl, 168bl.

TSÉ TSÉ AT GALERIE SENTOU
26 boulevard Raspail
75007 Paris
France
Tel: +33 1 45 49 00 05
and at
Maryse Boxer Design
26 Sloane Street
London SW1X 7QL, UK
Tel: +44 20 7 245 9493
Elegant, quirky lighting designs by a stylish young French company
Pages 49l, 130al.

URBAN RESEARCH LABORATORY
3 Plantain Place
Crosby Row
London SE1 1YN, UK
Tel: +44 20 7403 2929
jeff@urbanresearchlab.com
Pages 10, 16br, 127r, 134, 135bl, 139cl, 142br, 159br.

URBAN SALON
Architects
Unit D
Flat Iron Yard
Ayres Street
London SE1 1ES, UK
Tel: +44 20 7357 8000
Page 108bc.

VX DESIGN & ARCHITECTURE
www.vxdesign.com
vx@vxdesign.com
Tel/fax: +44 20 7370 5496
Pages 2ac, 2c, 4a, 18b, 28b, 32, 34l, 36br, 45ar, 55al, 75ar, 84, 85al, 129ac, 144al, 144ar, 157ar, 163a, 172cr, 173r.

STEPHEN VARADY ARCHITECTURE
Studio 5
102 Albion StreetSurry Hills
2010 Sydney
New South Wales
Australia
Tel: +61 2 9281 4825
Page 41b.

HÉRVE VERMESCH
50 rue Bichat
75010 Paris
France
Tel: +33 1 42 01 39 39
Pages 85ar, 146cl.

OLIVIER VIDAL AND ASSOCIATES (ARCHITECTS)
14 rue Moncey
75009 Paris
France
Pages 68a, 80bl.

BERNARD M. WHARTON
Shope Reno Wharton Associates
18 West Putnam Avenue
Greenwich CT 06830
Tel: 203 869 7250
srwol@aol.com
www.shoperenowharton.com
Page 94br.

HEIDI WISH AND PHILIP WISH
Interior Design & Build
Tel/fax: +44 207 737 7797
Pages 159ar, 162ar, 166ar.

VICENTE WOLF ASSOCIATES, INC.
333 West 39th Street
New York NY 10018
Tel: 212 465 0590
Page 94bl.

VOON WONG ARCHITECTS
Unit 27
1 Stannary Street
London SW11 4AD, UK
Tel: +44 20 7587 0116
Fax: +44 20 7840 0178
voon@dircon.co.uk
Pages 33al, 48, 138.

STEPHEN WOODHAM
Woodhams Ltd
Tel: +44 20 8964 9818
Pages 153bl, 154ar.

WOOLF ARCHITECTS
39–51 Highgate Road
London NW5 1RT, UK
Tel: +44 20 7428 9500
Pages 43b, 82b, 113cl, 115c.

YVES-CLAUDE DESIGN
Architectural/industrial design firm specializing in stainless-steel kitchens, furniture, and interiors
199 Layfayette Street
New York NY 10012
info@kanso.com
www.kanso.com
Pages 3l, 142c, 144br, 145cl, 145br, 149a, 153al, 153ac.

CONSUELO ZOELLY
5–7 rue Mont Louis
75011 Paris
France
Tel: +33 42 62 19 95
Page 142bl.

picture credits

All photographs by Chris Everard unless otherwise stated.
Key: ph=photographer, a=above, b=below, r=right, l=left, c=center.

1 Interior Designer Angela Kearsey's house in London-architectural design by Dols Wong Architects, interior design by Angela Kearsey; **2al** Hudson Street Loft designed by Moneo Brock Studio; **2ac** Ian Chee of VX design & architecture; **2ar&cl** Michael Nathenson's house in London; **2c** Ian Chee of VX design & architecture; **2cr** Interior Designer Angela Kearsey's house in London-architectural design by Dols Wong Architects, interior design by Angela Kearsey; **2bl** ph Alan Williams/Private apartment in London designed by Hugh Broughton Architects; **2br** ph Henry Bourne/Richard Mabb and Kate Green's apartment in London; **3l** Vicson Guevara's apartment in New York designed by Yves-Claude; **3c&r** Charles Bateson's house in London; **4a** Ian Chee of VX design & architecture; **4b** Nadav Kander & Nicole Verity's house; **5** A loft in London designed by Eger Architects; **6al** Hudson Street Loft designed by Moneo Brock Studio; **6ac** Charles Bateson's house in London; **6ar** ph Henry Bourne; **6cl** Ruth Artmonsky's loft in Covent Garden; **6bl** ph James Merrell; **6br** Interior Designer Angela Kearsey's house in London-architectural design by Dols Wong Architects, interior design by Angela Kearsey; **7a** Photographer Guy Hills' studio in London designed by Retrouvius; **7c** Designed by Filer & Cox, London; **7b** ph James Merrell/a house in Sydney designed by Interni Interior Design Consultancy; **8a** John Barman's Park Avenue Apartment; **8c** designed by Mullman Seidman Architects; **8b** Suze Orman's apartment in New York designed by Patricia Seidman of Mullman Seidman Architects; **9al** Nadav Kander & Nicole Verity's house; **9ar** a loft in London designed by Eger Architects; **9bl** ph Andrew Wood/A house in London designed by Bowles and Linares; **9bc** Freddie Daniells' apartment in London designed by Brookes Stacey Randall; **9cr** a house in Hampstead, London designed by Orefelt Associates; **9br** Charles Bateson's house in London; **10** ph Alan Williams/Richard Oyarzarbal's apartment in London designed by Urban Research Laboratory; **11al** A loft in London designed by Eger Architects; **11bl** ph James Morris/'The Peg Yorkin House' by Moore Ruble Yudell Architects & Planners. Principal in charge Buzz Yudell, Principal Designer John Ruble, Project Architect Marc Schoeplein; **11r** ph Tom Leighton/Sally Butler's house in London; **12** ph James Merrell/designed by Interni Interior Design Consultancy; **12–13** ph Henry Bourne/a house in London designed by Charles Rutherfoord; **13** ph Ray Main/Jonathan Leitersdorf's apartment in New York designed by Jonathan Leitersdorf/Just Design Ltd; **14al** ph Catherine Gratwicke/Johanne Riss' house in Brussels; **14ar** ph Andrew Wood/Pete & Connie di Girolamo house in San Diego; **14bl** The loft of Mary and Sean Kelly designed by Steven Learner Studio; **14bc** Dominique Lubar for IPL Interiors; **14br** Andrew Wood/Philip and Barbara Silver's house in Idaho designed by Mark Pynn A.I.A. of McMillen Pynn Architecture L.L.P.; **15l** ph Andrew Wood/Isosceles Land Pte Ltd's house in Singapore designed by Chan Soo Khian of SCDA Architects; **15c** ph Ray Main/Gisela Garson's house in Stoke Newington designed by FAT; **15r** ph Alan Williams/The Arbuthnott family's house near Cirencester designed by Nicholas Arbuthnott, fabrics designed by Vanessa Arbuthnott; **16a** Nadav Kander & Nicole Verity's house; **16bl** ph James Merrell/a house in Queensland designed by Tony Suttle; **16bc** ph Tom Leighton/Sally Butler's house in London; **16br** ph Alan Williams/Richard Oyarzarbal's apartment in London designed by Urban Research Laboratory; **17** ph Christopher Drake/Juan Corbella's apartment in London designed by HM2, Richard Webb with Andrew Hanson; **18al&r** Hudson Street Loft designed by Moneo Brock Studio; **18b** Ian Chee of VX design & architecture; **19al** John Barman's Park Avenue Apartment; **19ac&ar** Garden Room, London for David & Anne Harriss designed by Eger Architects; **19cl** Michael Nathenson's house in London; **19bl** Charles Bateson's house in London; **19br** Interior Designer Angela Kearsey's house in London-architectural design by Dols Wong Architects, interior design by Angela Kearsey; **20al** Michael Nathenson's house in London; **20ac** Suze Orman's apartment in New York designed by Patricia Seidman of Mullman Seidman Architects; **20ar** ph Andrew Wood/A house in London designed by Bowles and Linares; **20cl** Designed by Filer & Cox, London; **20c** A loft in London

designed by Eger Architects; **20cr** Michael Nathenson's house in London; **20bl** ph James Merrell/Sophie Sarin's flat in London; **20bc** ph James Merrell/Paula Pryke and Peter Romaniuk's house in London; **20br** ph David Montgomery/The Montevetro apartment in London designed by David Collins, photographed courtesy of Taylor Woodrow Capital Developments Ltd; **21a** ph James Merrell/Grant Ford and Jane Bailey's house in London/kitchen by Rhode Design; **21c** Charles Bateson's house in London; **21b** ph James Merrell/Sally Butler's house in London; **22** Photographer Guy Hills' studio in London designed by Retrouvius; **22–23** Nadav Kander & Nicole Verity's house; **23** The London apartment of the Sheppard Day Design Partnership; **24al** A loft in London designed by Eger Architects; **24ac** ph Alan Williams/Stanley & Nancy Grossman's apartment in New York designed by Jennifer Post Design; **24ar** ph James Morris/an atelier in Paris designed by Damien Roland; **24c** ph James Morris/'The Peg Yorkin House' by Moore Ruble Yudell Architects & Planners. Principal in charge Buzz Yudell, Principal Designer John Ruble, Project Architect Marc Schoeplein; **24b** ph James Morris/House in Harrison, New York, designed by Sidnam Petrone Gartner Architects; **25a** ph James Morris/A House in Wiltshire designed by Ken Shuttleworth; **25c** James Morris/A Mountain House in Georgia designed by Mack Scogin Merrill Elam Architects; **25b** ph Ray Main/Robert Callender & Elizabeth Ogilvie's studio in Fife designed by John C Hope Architects; **26a** ph James Morris/The Jackee' and Elgin Charles House in California's Hollywood Hills, designed by William R. Heffner AIA, interior design by Sandy Davidson Design; **26–27a** ph James Morris/The Lew House, originally designed by Richard Neutra in 1958, architect and contractor Marmol Radziner + Associates, Architecture and Construction; **26–27b** ph James Morris/Skywood House near London designed by Graham Phillips; **27** ph James Morris/Upper East Side Townhouse in New York City designed by Ogawa/Depardon Architects; **28al&ac** a loft in London designed by Eger Architects; **28ar** Photographer Guy Hills' studio in London designed by Retrouvius; **28b** Ian Chee of VX design & architecture; **29al** ph Ray Main/Jamie Falla's house in London designed by MOOArc; **29ar** ph James Morris/House refurbishment in North London, Mark Guard Architects; **29br** Charles Bateson's house in London; **30al** ph Ray Main/Jonathan Reed's apartment in London; **30c** Ray Main/an apartment in London designed by Brookes Stacey Randall; **30ar** Garden Room, London for David & Anne Harriss designed by Eger Architects; **30bl** ph Andrew Wood/Namly Drive house in Singapore designed by Juan Peck Foon; **30br** Ruth Artmonsky's loft in Covent Garden; **31** ph Ray Main/an apartment in London designed by Brookes Stacey Randall; **32** Ian Chee of VX design & architecture; **33al** ph Alan Williams/The architect Voon Wong's own apartment in London; **33bl** ph Henry Bourne/Frédéric Méchiche's apartment in Paris; **33r** ph Catherine Gratwicke/Agnès Emery's house in Brussels, tiles from Emery & Cie; **34l** Ian Chee of VX design & architecture; **34c** ph Henry Bourne/a house in Devon designed by Anthony Hudson of Hudson Featherstone Architects; **34–35** ph Ray Main/Client's residence, East Hampton, New York, designed by ZG DESIGN; **35al** ph James Merrell/an apartment in New York designed by Campion A Platt Architect; **35ar** ph Henry Bourne/Linda Trahair's house in Bath; **35c&bl** Photographer Guy Hills' studio in London designed by Retrouvius; **35br** ph Ray Main/Thierry Watorek's house near Paris; **36al** ph Henry Bourne/Felix Bonnier's apartment in New York; **36ar** Charles Bateson's house in London; **36bl** ph James Merrell/a house in Sydney designed by Luigi Rosselli; **36br** Ian Chee of VX design & architecture; **37a** ph Henry Bourne/a mews house in London designed by McDowell & Benedetti; **37b** ph Henry Bourne; **38al&br** ph Henry Bourne; **38ar** ph James Merrell; **38bl** ph James Merrell/a house in London designed by François Gilles & Dominique Lubar, IPL Interiors; **38–39 & 39bl** James Merrell/a terrace in London designed by Christophe Gollut; **39ar** ph Catherine Gratwicke/Agnès Emery's house in Brussels, tiles from Emery & Cie; **39br** ph James Merrell/a house in Sydney designed by Interni Interior Design Consultancy; **40** ph James Morris/an atelier in Paris designed by Damien Roland; **41a** ph Henry Bourne/a mews house in London designed by Architect McDowell & Benedetti; **41c** ph Henry Bourne/Charles Rutherfoord's house in London; **41b** ph James Merrell/Amanda and Andrew Manning's apartment in Sydney designed by Stephen Varady Architecture; **42al** ph Ray Main/Robert Callender & Elizabeth Ogilvie's studio in Fife designed by John C Hope Architects; **42ar** ph Henry Bourne/a loft in London designed by Robert Dye Associates; **42b** ph Henry Bourne/DAD Associates; **43a** ph Henry Bourne/a house in

London designed by Mark Guard Architects; **43b** ph Henry Bourne/a house in London designed by Woolf architects; **44** Designed by Filer & Cox, London; **45al** a loft in London designed by Eger Architects; **45ac** ph Henry Bourne/Frédéric Méchiche's apartment in Paris; **45ar** Ian Chee of VX design & architecture; **45b** Henry Bourne/a house in Devon designed by Anthony Hudson of Hudson Featherstone Architects; **46a** all Henry Bourne/a house in London designed by Charles Rutherfoord; **46bl** Ray Main/Thierry Watorek's house near Paris; **46br** ph James Merrell; **47** Nadav Kander & Nicole Verity's house; **48** ph Alan Williams/The architect Voon Wong's own apartment in London; **49l** ph Ray Main/lights by Tsé Tsé associées, Catherine Levy and Sigolène Prébois; **49c** ph Ray Main/Evan Snyderman's house in Brooklyn; **49r** ph Alan Williams/Jennifer & Geoffrey Symonds' apartment in New York designed by Jennifer Post Design; **50al** Andrew Wilson's apartment in London designed by Azman Owens; **50ar** ph Alan Williams/Private apartment in London designed by Hugh Broughton Architects; **50b** ph James Merrell/Victor Ktori's loft in London designed by Circus Architects; **51** Designer Karim Rashid's own apartment in New York; **52al** ph Henry Bourne/John Raab's apartment in London/floor by Sinclair Till; **52ar** ph Henry Bourne/a house in London designed by Charles Rutherfoord; **52bl** ph James Merrell/Sue and Andy's apartment in Blackheath; **52br** ph Henry Bourne/an apartment in London designed by Emily Todhunter; **53al** ph Henry Bourne/Dan and Claire Thorne's town house in Dorset designed by Sarah Featherstone of Hudson Featherstone Architects; **53ar** ph Henry Bourne/floor by Dalsouple, First Floor; **53bl** ph Henry Bourne/Circus Architects/floor by First Floor; **53br** ph Henry Bourne/Richard Mabb and Kate Green's apartment in London; **54al** ph Henry Bourne/Roger and Fay Oates' house in Eastnor; **54ac** ph James Merrell/rug designed by Christine Vanderhurd; **54ar** ph James Merrell; **54cr** ph Andrew Wood/Roger and Fay Oates' house in Eastnor; **54–55b** ph Henry Bourne/floor by Helen Yardley; **55al** Ian Chee of VX design & architecture; **55ar** Charles Bateson's house in London; **55cr** ph James Merrell; **55br** ph Henry Bourne/an apartment in London designed by Ash Sakula Architects/rug by Christopher Farr; **56** ph Andrew Wood/Roger and Suzy Black's apartment in London designed by Johnson Naylor; **57l** ph Ray Main/a loft in London designed by Circus Architects; **57c** ph Andrew Wood/Phil and Gail Handy's house in Idaho designed by Mark Pynn A.I.A. of McMillen Pynn Architecture L.L.P.; **57r** ph James Morris/a house near Brussels designed by Claire Bataille & Paul ibens; **58** ph Andrew Wood/Alastair Hendy & John Clinch's apartment in London designed by Alastair Hendy; **58–59** ph Andrew Wood/Nik Randall, Suzsi Corio and Louis' home in London designed by Brookes Stacey Randall; **59** Photographer Guy Hills' studio in London designed by Retrouvius; **60al&cl** ph Ray Main/a loft in London designed by Circus Architects; **60bl** ph Ray Main/Seth Stein's house in London; **60r** ph James Morris/a house near Brussels designed by Claire Bataille & Paul ibens; **61ar** ph Ray Main/an apartment in London designed by Circus Architects; **61c** An apartment in New York designed by Gabellini Associates; **61bl&br** John Eldridge's loft apartment in London designed by Seth Stein; **62l** ph Andrew Wood; **62r** ph Ray Main/David Mellor's home and studio at Hathersage in Derbyshire; **62–63** ph Ray Main/Kenneth Hirst's apartment in New York; **64al** ph Andrew Wood/Phil and Gail Handy's house in Idaho designed by Mark Pynn A.I.A. of McMillen Pynn Architecture L.L.P.; **64ar** ph James Morris/Nomentana Residence in Maine designed by Mack Scogin Merrill Elam Architects; **64bl** ph Andrew Wood/an apartment in Bath designed by Briffa Phillips Architects; **64bc** ph Andrew Wood/Media executive's house in Los Angeles, Architect: Stephen Slan, Builder: Ken Duran, Furnishings: Russell Simpson, Original Architect: Carl Maston c.1945; **64br** ph Ray Main/John Howell's loft in London designed by Circus Architects; **65** ph Ray Main/a loft in London designed by Circus Architects; **66a&cr** ph Andrew Wood/An apartment in London designed by James Gorst; **66cl** ph Andrew Wood/Roger and Suzy Black's apartment in London designed by Johnson Naylor; **66b** ph Tom Leighton/armoire & chair Josephine Ryan; **67al** ph Ray Main/Mr & Mrs Cordier's home, Church Farm Oast, near Horsmonden, Kent, UK; **67ar** ph Andrew Wood/Richard and Sue Hare's house in Idaho designed by Mark Pynn A.I.A. of McMillen Pynn Architecture L.L.P.; **67bl** ph Chris Tubbs/Nickerson-Wakefield House in upstate New York/anderson architects; **67br** ph Ray Main/Marina & Peter Hill's barn in West Sussex designed by Marina Hill, Peter James Construction Management, Chichester, The West Sussex Antique Timber Company, Wisborough Green, and Joanna Jefferson Architects;

68a&b ph James Merrell; **68–69** ph Andrew Wood/Media executive's house in Los Angeles, Architect: Stephen Slan, Builder: Ken Duran, Furnishings: Russell Simpson, Original Architect: Carl Maston c. 1945; **70a** ph Alan Williams/Andrew Wallace's house in London; **70c** ph Tom Leighton; **70b** ph Alan Williams/Interior Designer Roberto Bergero's own apartment in Paris; **71a** all Dominique Lubar for IPL Interiors; **71cl** François Muracciole's apartment in Paris; **71bl** ph Andrew Wood/an apartment in The San Remo on the Upper West Side of Manhattan, designed by John L. Stewart and Michael D'Arcy of SIT; **71br** Nadav Kander & Nicole Verity's house; **72al&bl** Designed by Filer & Cox, London; **72ac&ar** ph Alan Williams/Katie Bassford King's house in London designed by Touch Interior Design; **73al** ph Ray Main/a house in Pennsylvania designed by Jeffrey Bilhuber; **73bl** Designed by Filer & Cox, London; **73a&br & 74** Nadav Kander & Nicole Verity's house; **75l** ph James Morris/a house in London designed by Alan Power; **75ar** Ian Chee of VX design & architecture; **75br** ph Ray Main/Lee F. Mindel's apartment in New York, designed by Shelton, Mindel & Associates with Associate Architect Reed Morrison, lighting design by Johnson Schwinghammer; **76a** ph James Morris/Upper East Side Townhouse in New York City designed by Ogawa/Depardon Architects; **76b** ph James Morris/a house in London designed by Alan Power; **77** ph Ray Main/Lee F. Mindel's apartment in New York, designed by Shelton, Mindel & Associates with Associate Architect Reed Morrison, lighting design by Johnson Schwinghammer; **78l** ph Ray Main/an apartment in London designed by Circus Architects; **78r** ph James Morris/The Jackee' and Elgin Charles House in California's Hollywood Hills, designed by William R. Heffner AIA, interior design by Sandy Davidson Design; **79 both** ph James Morris/Upper East Side Townhouse in New York City designed by Ogawa/Depardon Architects; **80bl** ph James Merrell; **80bc** Ruth Artmonsky's loft in Covent Garden; **80a&br** Nadav Kander & Nicole Verity's house; **81l** ph James Morris/The Lew House, originally designed by Richard Neutra in 1958, architect and contractor Marmol Radziner + Associates, Architecture and Construction **81r** Photographer Guy Hills' studio in London designed by Retrouvius; **82a** ph Henry Bourne/a house in Devon designed by Anthony Hudson of Hudson Featherstone Architects; **82b** ph Henry Bourne/a house in London designed by Woolf architects; **83** ph James Morris/a house in London designed by Alan Power; **84 & 85al** Ian Chee of VX design & architecture; **85ac** ph Ray Main/Lee F. Mindel's apartment in New York, designed by Shelton, Mindel & Associates with Associate Architect Reed Morrison, lighting design by Johnson Schwinghammer; **85ar** ph Ray Main/a house in Paris designed by Hervé Vermesch; **85c** ph Ray Main/Kirk & Caroline Pickering's house in London, space creation by Square Foot Properties Ltd; **85cr** ph Ray Main/Mr & Mrs Cordier's home, Church Farm Oast, near Horsmonden, Kent, UK; **85br** ph Ray Main/Robert Callender & Elizabeth Ogilvie's studio in Fife designed by John C Hope Architects; **86l** ph Andrew Wood/Jamie Falla's house in London designed by MOOArc; **86ar&br** ph Andrew Wood/a house near Antwerp designed by Claire Bataille and Paul ibens; **87** ph Henry Bourne/a house in Devon designed by Anthony Hudson of Hudson Featherstone Architects; **88** Hudson Street Loft designed by Moneo Brock Studio; **89al** Dominique Lubar for IPL Interiors; **89bl** Suze Orman's apartment in New York designed by Patricia Seidman of Mullman Seidman Architects; **89c&r** Michael Nathenson's house in London; **90** Charles Bateson's house in London; **91al** Interior Designer Angela Kearsey's house in London-architectural design by Dols Wong Architects, interior design by Angela Kearsey; **91ar** ph Andrew Wood/An apartment in London designed by James Gorst; **91bl** The London apartment of the Sheppard Day Design Partnership; **91bc** ph Andrew Wood/Jamie Falla's house in London designed by MOOArc; **91br** Dominique Lubar for IPL Interiors; **92 & 93al** Michael Nathenson's house in London; **93ar** Hudson Street Loft designed by Moneo Brock Studio; **93br** Nadav Kander & Nicole Verity's house; **94a** ph Polly Wreford/Sheila Scholes & Gunter Schmidt's house in Cambridgeshire; **94bl** ph Ray Main/a house in East Hampton, interior by Vicente Wolf; **94br** ph Chris Tubbs/A cottage in Connecticut designed by Benard M. Wharton; **95** Dominique Lubar for IPL Interiors; **96al** ph Andrew Wood/The Glendale, California, home of John & Heather Banfield; **96bl** ph Alan Williams/Katie Bassford King's house in London designed by Touch Interior Design; **96—97** ph Alan Williams/Owner of Gloss, Pascale Bredillet's own apartment in London; **97** ph Alan Williams/Warner Johnson's apartment in New York designed by Edward Cabot of Cabot Design Ltd.; **98al** ph Andrew Wood/Evelyne Roussel's house in Paris; **98ac**

PICTURE CREDITS

Photographer Guy Hills' studio in London designed by Retrouvius; **98ar** Suze Orman's apartment in New York designed by Patricia Seidman of Mullman Seidman Architects; **98b** both a loft in London designed by Eger Architects; **99a** ph Andrew Wood/an apartment in Knokke, Belgium designed by Claire Bataille and Paul ibens; **99b** ph Ray Main/Mr & Mrs Cordier's home, Church Farm Oast, near Horsmonden, Kent, UK; **100al** Freddie Daniells' apartment in London designed by Brookes Stacey Randall; **100ar** Charles Bateson's house in London; **100b** Dominique Lubar for IPL Interiors; **101al** Nadav Kander & Nicole Verity's house; **101ar** ph Ray Main/Darren and Sheila Chadwick's apartment in London designed by Sergisson Bates; **101b** ph Andrew Wood/Alastair Hendy & John Clinch's apartment in London designed by Alastair Hendy; **102a** ph Chris Tubbs/Mike Taitt's railway carriage in Scotland; **102b** ph Chris Tubbs/Jonathan Adler's and Simon Doonan's house on Shelter Island near New York designed by Schefer Design; **103al** ph Jan Baldwin/Compound by a lakeside in the mountains of western Maine designed by Stephen Blatt Architects; **103bl** ph Jan Baldwin/Interior Designer Philip Hooper's own house in East Sussex; **103ar** ph James Merrell; **103br** ph Tom Leighton; **104** Michael Nathenson's house in London; **105al** Designed by Mullman Seidman Architects; **105ar** ph Andrew Wood/Paula Pryke and Peter Romaniuk's house in London; **105bl** An apartment in Milan designed by Nicoletta Marazza; **105br** Michael Nathenson's house in London; **106a** Sig.ra Venturini's apartment in Milan; **106bl** David Mullman's apartment in New York designed by Mullman Seidman Architects; **106br** Apartment in Antwerp designed by Claire Bataille & Paul ibens; **106—107** Ruth Artmonsky's loft in Covent Garden; **108a** Charles Bateson's house in London; **108c** Michael Nathenson's house in London; **108bl** Dominique Lubar for IPL Interiors; **108bc** ph Andrew Wood/Rosa Dean & Ed Baden-Powell's apartment in London, designed by Urban Salon (020 7357 8800); **108br & 109** Michael Nathenson's house in London; **110br&a** both Michael Nathenson's house in London; **110bl** Andrew Wood/Paula Pryke and Peter Romaniuk's house in London; **111cl&a** both ph Andrew Wood/a house in London designed by François Gilles and Dominique Lubar, IPL Interiors; **111bl** ph Andrew Wood/a house in London designed by Guy Stansfeld (020 7727 0133); **111br** Interior Designer Angela Kearsey's house in London-architectural design by Dols Wong Architects, interior design by Angela Kearsey; **112** Designed by Mullman Seidman Architects; **113al** The loft of Mary and Sean Kelly designed by Steven Learner Studio; **113cl** ph Andrew Wood/David Jermyn's house in London, designed by Woolf Architects (020 7428 9500); **113bl** ph Polly Wreford/Marie-Hélène de Taillac's pied-à-terre in Paris; **113ar** ph Andrew Wood/Chelsea Studio New York City, designed by Marino + Giolito; **113br** Interior Designer Angela Kearsey's house in London-architectural design by Dols Wong Architects, interior design by Angela Kearsey; **114** ph Andrew Wood/a house in London designed by Guy Stansfeld (020 7727 0133); **115al** An apartment in Milan designed by Nicoletta Marazza; **115ac** Bob & Maureen Macris' apartment on Fifth Avenue in New York designed by Sage Wimer Coombe Architects; **115ar** ph David Montgomery/Sheila Scholes & Gunter Schmidt's house in Cambridgeshire; **115c** ph Andrew Wood/David Jermyn's house in London, designed by Woolf Architects (020 7428 9500); **115b** ph Andrew Wood; **116** ph Ray Main/Lee F. Mindel's apartment in New York, lighting designed by Johnson Schwinghammer, light from Mobilier; **117l** François Muracciole's apartment in Paris; **117ac** ph Ray Main/light by Artemide; **117bc** Ruth Artmonsky's loft in Covent Garden; **117r & 118al** Dominique Lubar for IPL Interiors; **118bl** ph Ray Main/Seth Stein's house in London; **118—119** ph James Morris/Skywood House near London designed by Graham Phillips; **119a** ph Ray Main/an apartment in London designed by Circus Architects, lights from SKK; **119b** ph Ray Main/Jonathan Reed's apartment in London, lighting designed by Sally Storey, Design Director of John Cullen Lighting; **120al** ph Ray Main/Darren and Sheila Chadwick's apartment in London designed by Sergisson Bates; **120ac** Interior Designer Angela Kearsey's house in London-architectural design by Dols Wong Architects, interior design by Angela Kearsey; **120ar** ph Andrew Wood/The Shell House, California, home of Chuck and Evelyn Plemons; **120cl** ph Andrew Wood/Randell L. Makinson house, Pasadena, California. Design: Buff & Hensman FAIA & Randall L. Makinson, Hon. AIA, Associated Architects; **120cr** ph Ray Main/an apartment in New York designed by Laura Bohn Design Associates Inc., light from Lightforms; **120bl** ph Ray Main/Seth Stein's house in London, wall light by Serge Mouille; **120br &121** Interior Designer Angela

Kearsey's house in London-architectural design by Dols Wong Architects, interior design by Angela Kearsey; **122al** ph Ray Main/John Howell's loft in London designed by Circus Architects; **122ar&cl** Ruth Artmonsky's loft in Covent Garden; **122bl** ph Ray Main/an apartment in New York designed by Laura Bohn Design Associates Inc.; **122bc** Garden Room, London for David & Anne Harriss designed by Eger Architects; **122br** ph Ray Main/Mark Jennings' apartment in New York designed by Asfour Guzy; **123a** ph Ray Main/Seth Stein's house in London, light by Erco; **123bl** Dominique Lubar for IPL Interiors; **123br** ph Ray Main/a loft in London designed by Nico Rensch, light from SKK; **124l** ph Ray Main; **124r** Suze Orman's apartment in New York designed by Patricia Seidman of Mullman Seidman Architects; **125ar&ac** ph Ray Main/Malin Iovino's apartment in London; **125ar&cl** ph Ray Main; **125bl** ph Ray Main/light by Erco; **125br** ph Alan Williams/Jennifer & Geoffrey Symonds' apartment in New York designed by Jennifer Post Design; **126al** Dominique Lubar for IPL Interiors; **126ac** ph James Merrell/Andrew Arnott and Karin Schack's house in Melbourne, Australia; **126ar** ph Andrew Wood/Duncan-Irwin House in Pasadena, California, home of André & Ann Chaves; **126bl** ph Andrew Wood/The King House in Mammoth Lakes, California; **126bc** ph Ray Main/light from Hector Finch; **126br** ph Ray Main/light by Louis Poulsen; **127l** both designed by Mullman Seidman Architects; **127r** ph Alan Williams/Richard Oyarzarbal's apartment in London designed by Urban Research Laboratory; **128** ph Ray Main/a loft in London designed by Nico Rensch, light from SKK; **129al** ph Ray Main/light by Artemide; **129ac** Ian Chee of VX design & architecture; **129ar** ph Ray Main/a loft in London designed by Circus Architects, light from Fulham Kitchens; **129bl** ph Andrew Wood/The Glendale, California, home of John & Heather Banfield; **129bc** ph Ray Main/Jonathan Reed's apartment in London, light by Best & Lloyd; **129br** ph Ray Main/a house in London designed by Ash Sakula Architects, light from Habitat; **130al** ph Ray Main/lighting by Tsé Tsé associées, Catherine Levy and Sigolène Prébois, **130ar** ph Ray Main/a house in Pennsylvania designed by Jeffrey Bilhuber, light by Isamu Noguchi; **130bl** ph Ray Main/Lee F. Mindel's apartment in New York, designed by Shelton, Mindel & Associates with Associate Architect Reed Morrison, lighting design by Johnson Schwinghammer; **130br** ph Ray Main/light from Ecart International; **131a** ph Ray Main/a loft in London designed by Nico Rensch; **131b** Ray Main/light from The Conran Shop; **132a** ph Ray Main/light from Babylon Design; **132bl** ph Andrew Wood/The Caroline Deforest House in Pasadena, California, home of Michael Murray and Kelly Jones; **132br** ph Andrew Wood/The King House in Mammoth Lakes, California; **133al** François Muracciole's apartment in Paris; **133ar&br** ph Andrew Wood/The Glendale, California, home of John & Heather Banfield; **133bl** ph Ray Main/light from Mathmos; **133bc** ph Ray Main/light by Charlotte Packe from Space; **134 & 135bl** ph Alan Williams/Richard Oyarzarbal's apartment in London designed by Urban Research Laboratory; **135al&ac** ph Ray Main; **135ar** ph Ray Main/Gai Harris' apartment in London designed by François Gilles and Dominique Lubar of IPL Interiors; **135bc** Dominique Lubar for IPL Interiors; **135br** Suze Orman's apartment in New York designed by Patricia Seidman of Mullman Seidman Architects; **136** John Barman's Park Avenue Apartment; **137al&bl** Michael Nathenson's house in London; **137ar** designed by Mullman Seidman Architects; **137c** Designer Karim Rashid's own apartment in New York; **137br** ph Alan Williams/Private apartment in London designed by Hugh Broughton Architects; **138** ph Alan Williams/The architect Voon Wong's own apartment in London; **139al** ph Andrew Wood/a house in London designed by Orefelt Associates, Design team Gunnar Orefelt and Knut Hovland; **139ar** ph James Merrell/Douglas and Dorothy Hamilton's apartment in New York; **139cl** ph Alan Williams/Richard Oyarzarbal's apartment in London designed by Urban Research Laboratory; **139c** ph Ray Main/Kenneth Hirst's apartment in New York; **139cr** ph Andrew Wood/A house in London designed by Bowles and Linares; **139bl** ph Andrew Wood/Robert Kimsey's apartment in London designed by Gavin Jackson (07050 097561); **139bc** ph Andrew Wood/Paula Pryke and Peter Romaniuk's house in London; **139br** ph James Merrell; **140l** ph Andrew Wood/Neil Bingham's house in Blackheath, London; **140ar** ph Andrew Wood; **140cr** Hudson Street Loft designed by Moneo Brock Studio; **140br** Suze Orman's apartment in New York designed by Patricia Seidman of Mullman Seidman Architects; **141al** designed by Mullman Seidman Architects; **141bl** The loft of Mary and Sean Kelly designed by Steven Learner Studio; **141r** Michael Nathenson's house in London;

142a ph Alan Williams/Maria Jesus Polanco's apartment in New York designed by Hut Sachs Studio in collaboration with Moneo Brock Studio; **142cl** ph James Merrell/kitchen by Rhode Design; **142c** Vicson Guevara's apartment in New York designed by Yves-Claude; **142cr** Designed by Filer & Cox, London; **142bl** ph James Merrell/Consuelo Zoelly's apartment in Paris; **142bc** Charles Bateson's house in London; **142br** ph Alan Williams/Richard Oyarzarbal's apartment in London designed by Urban Research Laboratory; **143a** Suze Orman's apartment in New York designed by Patricia Seidman of Mullman Seidman Architects; **143b** designed by Mullman Seidman Architects; **144al&ar** Ian Chee of VX design & architecture; **144br** Vicson Guevara's apartment in New York designed by Yves-Claude; **145al** ph Alan Williams/Private apartment in London designed by Hugh Broughton Architects; **145ar** Designer Karim Rashid's own apartment in New York; **145bl** John Barman's Park Avenue Apartment; **145cl&br** Vicson Guevara's apartment in New York designed by Yves-Claude; **146al** ph James Merrell/a house in London designed by Ash Sakula Architects; **146ac** ph Christopher Drake/Melanie Thornton's house in Gloucestershire; **146ar** ph James Merrell; **146cl** ph James Merrell/an apartment in Paris designed by Hervé Vermesch; **146c** ph Ray Main/Marie Pierre Morel's house in Paris designed by François Muracciole; **146cr** Sig.ra Venturini's apartment in Milan; **146bl** ph James Merrell/Felix Bonnier's apartment in Paris; **146bc** ph James Merrell/Sophie Sarin's flat in London; **146br** ph Andrew Wood/Curtice Booth's house in Pasadena, California; **147a** Hudson Street Loft designed by Moneo Brock Studio; **147c** ph Christopher Drake/Refurbishment and interior design by Chicchi Meroni Fassio, Parnassus; **147b** ph James Merrell/Sussie Ahlburg and Andy Keate's house in London; **148al** ph Polly Wreford/Lena Proudlock's house in Gloucestershire; **148bl** François Muracciole's apartment in Paris; **148r** Suze Orman's apartment in New York designed by Patricia Seidman of Mullman Seidman Architects; **149l** Michael Nathenson's house in London; **149a** Vicson Guevara's apartment in New York designed by Yves-Claude; **149br** Kampfner's house in London designed by Ash Sakula Architects; **150a,bl&bc** John Barman's Park Avenue Apartment; **150br** ph Andrew Wood; **151al&ac** Hudson Street Loft designed by Moneo Brock Studio **151ar** Arlene Hirst's New York Kitchen designed by Steven Sclaroff; **151b** Designer Karim Rashid's own apartment in New York; **152a** John Barman's Park Avenue Apartment; **152bl** ph James Merrell/Mike and Kris Taylor's loft in London designed by Circus Architects with Kayode Lipede; **152br** designed by Mullman Seidman Architects; **153al&ac** Vicson Guevara's apartment in New York designed by Yves-Claude; **153ar** Michael Nathenson's house in London; **153cl** Hudson Street Loft designed by Moneo Brock Studio; **153bl** ph James Merrell/Stephen Woodham's house in London designed in conjunction with Mark Brook Design; **153br** designed by Mullman Seidman Architects; **154al** ph Alan Williams/The Arbuthnott family's house near Cirencester designed by Nicholas Arbuthnott, fabrics designed by Vanessa Arbuthnott; **154ac** ph James Merrell/Ash Sakula's house in London; **154ar** ph James Merrell/Stephen Woodham's house in London designed in conjunction with Mark Brook Design; **154bl** Designed by Filer & Cox, London; **154–155b & 155c** Hudson Street Loft designed by Moneo Brock Studio; **155al** Arlene Hirst's New York Kitchen designed by Steven Sclaroff; **155ac** a house in London designed by Ash Sakula Architects; **155ar** ph James Merrell/Linda Parham and David Slobham's apartment in Sydney designed by architect Stephen Varady; **155b** ph James Merrell/Rose Gray's flat in London designed by Hester Gray; **156** a house in Hampstead, London designed by Orefelt Associates; **157al** John Barman's Park Avenue Apartment; **157ac** Designed by Filer & Cox, London; **157ar** Ian Chee of VX design & architecture; **157b** designed by Mullman Seidman Architects; **158al** ph James Morris/A house in London designed by Azman Owens Architects; **158ar** Philippa Rose's house in London designed by Caroline Paterson/Victoria Fairfax of Paterson Gornall Interiors, together with Clive Butcher Designs; **158cl** ph Henry Bourne/a house in London designed by Charles Rutherfoord; **158bl** ph Andrew Wood/An apartment in London designed by James Gorst; **158br** Charles Bateson's house in London; **159l** Calvin Tsao & Zack McKown's apartment in New York designed by Tsao & McKown; **159ar** Heidi Wish & Philip Wish's apartment in London designed by Moutarde & Heidi Wish; **159br** ph Alan Williams/Richard Oyarzarbal's apartment in London designed by Urban Research Laboratory; **160a** ph Alan Williams/Hudson Street Loft in New York designed by Moneo Brock Studio; **160cl** Karen Davies' apartment in London designed by Joëlle Darby;

160bl John Eldridge's loft apartment in London designed by Seth Stein; **160bc** an apartment in Paris designed by Bruno Tanquerel; **160br** One New Inn Square, a private dining room and home of chef David Vanderhook, all enquiries (020 7729 3645); **161a** ph James Morris/'The Jackee' and Elgin Charles House in California's Hollywood Hills, designed by William R. Heffner AIA, interior design by Sandy Davidson Design; **161bl** ph James Morris/A loft apartment in London designed by Simon Conder Associates; **161bc** The London apartment of the Sheppard Day Design Partnership; **161br** a house in Hampstead, London designed by Orefelt Associates; **162al** Michael Nathenson's house in London; **162ac** Freddie Daniells' apartment in London designed by Brookes Stacey Randall; **162ar** Heidi Wish & Philip Wish's apartment in London designed by Moutarde & Heidi Wish; **162bl** a house in Hampstead, London designed by Orefelt Associates; **162cr** House in London by Seth Stein; **162br** Designed by Filer & Cox, London; **163a** Ian Chee of VX design & architecture; **163b** Calvin Tsao & Zack McKown's apartment in New York designed by Tsao & McKown; **164l** Emma & Neil's house in London, walls painted by Garth Carter; **164r** A loft apartment in London designed by Simon Conder Associates; **165al** Suzanne Slesin & Michael Steinberg's apartment in New York – design by Jean-Louis Ménard; **165cl** Calvin Tsao & Zack McKown's apartment in New York designed by Tsao & McKown; **165bl** a house in Highbury, London designed by Dale Loth Architects; **165ar** John Barman's Park Avenue Apartment; **165bc** architect's house in London designed by Dale Loth Architects; **165br** Simon Brignall & Christina Rosetti's loft apartment in London designed by David Mikhail Architects; **166al** New York City apartment designed by Marino + Giolito; **166ac** Charles Bateson's house in London; **166ar** Heidi Wish & Philip Wish's apartment in London designed by Moutarde & Heidi Wish; **166cl** Richard Hopkin's apartment in London designed by HM2; **166c** an apartment in New York designed by David Deutsch & Sidnam Petrone Gartner Architects; **166cr** Architect Nigel Smith's apartment in London; **166bl** One New Inn Square, a private dining room and home of chef David Vanderhook, all enquiries (020 7729 3645); **166bc&br** a house in Paris designed by Bruno Tanquerel; **167a** Hudson Street Loft designed by Moneo Brock Studio; **167c** Nadav Kander & Nicole Verity's house; **167b & 168al** John Eldridge's loft apartment in London designed by Seth Stein; **168ar** Charles Bateson's house in London; **168bl** Calvin Tsao & Zack McKown's apartment in New York designed by Tsao & McKown; **168br** Paul Brazier & Diane Lever's house in London designed by Carden & Cunietti; **169al** a house in Paris designed by Bruno Tanquerel; **169ac** ph Andrew Wood/Alastair Hendy & John Clinch's apartment in London designed by Alastair Hendy; **169ar** Sera Hersham-Loftus' house in London; **169cr** architect's house in London designed by Dale Loth Architects; **169br** a house in London designed by Carden & Cunietti; **170al** Simon Brignall & Christina Rosetti's loft apartment in London designed by David Mikhail Architects; **170ar** a house in Hampstead, London designed by Orefelt Associates; **170c** New York City apartment designed by Marino + Giolito; **170b** Designed by Filer & Cox, London; **171al** Jacques & Laurence Hintzy's apartment near Paris designed by Paul Mathieu; **171ac** Michael Nathenson's house in London; **171ar** Suze Orman's apartment in New York designed by Patricia Seidman of Mullman Seidman Architects; **171b** designed by Mullman Seidman Architects; **172al** ph Andrew Wood/A house at Jalan Berjaya, Singapore designed by Chan Soo Khian of SCDA Architects; **172ac** ph Andrew Wood/Roger and Suzy Black's apartment in London designed by Johnson Naylor; **172ar** Michael Nathenson's house in London; **172cl** Gentucca Bini's apartment in Milan; **172c** ph Henry Bourne/a loft in London designed by DAD Associates; **172cr** Ian Chee of VX design & architecture; **172bl** Designed by Filer & Cox, London; **172bc** ph Andrew Wood/A house near Antwerp designed by Claire Bataille and Paul ibens; **172br** ph Andrew Wood/Media executive's house in Los Angeles, Architect: Stephen Slan, Builder: Ken Duran, Furnishings: Russell Simpson, Original Architect: Carl Maston c. 1945; **173l** Suze Orman's apartment in New York designed by Patricia Seidman of Mullman Seidman Architects; **173c** ph Alan Williams/Alannah Weston's house in London designed by Stickland Coombe Architecture; **173r** Ian Chee of VX design & architecture.

In addition to the designers and owners mentioned above we would also like to thank Katsuji Asada and garden antiques expert Peter Hone.

189

index

DESIGNS ON INGENUITY

MAKING LIFE EASIER, SIMPLER AND MORE RELAXING AT HOME

Protection against the onslaught of toothpaste; defense against shaving cream and soap scum—the innovative EverClean™ Faucet Finish from American Standard makes cleaning faucets child's play.

That's because faucets with the EverClean Finish are spot-free with one wipe and without cleaning products so bath and kitchen faucets will look and stay cleaner—between cleanings. The patented permanent finish will last the life of the faucet and the broad range of styles and finishes means there's one just right for your home.

American Standard bathroom faucets also feature the Speed Connect™ drain. With one third the parts of a traditional drain it's the world's fastest to install.

EverClean

Metal

Finish

Reliant+™ Kitchen Faucet

One™ Bathroom Sink Faucet

The American Standard Ingenuity Tour coming soon! Touring showrooms containing the latest American Standard products are coming to a location near you. In addition to the EverClean Faucet Finish technology, you can see to lets that are virtually clog-free and help keep themselves clean, drains that require no tools, whirlpools with Comfort Jets™ and much more. Visit **www.americanstandard-us.com** for dates and locations.

American Standard

its production to distillates of blue agave grown in 5 of Mexico's 31 states. Crowley and DeJoria ultimately concluded that the best blue agave terroir was in the state of Jalisco, in the highlands east of Guadalajara.

"Taste this," says Francisco Alcarez, Patrón's master blender, handing me a fibrous piece of cooked agave fresh out of the brick oven at the Patrón plant. It's very sweet, of course, with a distinctive taste like roasted, resinous mango. "That's what tequila should taste like." A wiry bantamweight with a hatlike thatch of shiny dark hair, Alcarez is taking me through the production facilities inside the new Patrón headquarters, a sprawling reproduction of the sort of eclectic Franco-Italianate hacienda that one of the old Spanish families might have built a couple of hundred years ago.

After the agave is crushed and fermented, the juice is distilled twice in a copper still, emerging from the second distillation at 80 proof (40 percent alcohol). Pure agave tequila still tastes like agave when it emerges from the still, and if the agave is of the highest quality, this is presumably a good thing. Some grades of tequila then spend time in a barrel—*reposado* (at least two months) and *añejo* (at least one year)—before they go off to Patrón's bottling line, where two shifts of more than a hundred people label and cork the handblown bottles.

I've always preferred Patrón's unaged silver (*blanco*) to the ostensibly higher grades, and now I know why. I like the taste of agave, apparently, more than I like the taste of barrels, a preference I share with Ajendra Singh, the cosmopolitan head of production at Patrón. "Silver is the way to really taste the agave," says Singh, handing me a small, room-temperature brandy snifter of the $200-a-bottle Gran Patrón after my tour.

The smokier, woodier *añejo* and *reposado* tequilas have their virtues and admirers. Derek Sanders, co-owner of Manhattan's subterranean La Esquina, prefers the smokier, richer taste of the *reposados* and *añejos*. He likes his tequila straight, or with a *sangrita* chaser composed of tomato and orange juices spiked with chilies. At the moment he particularly likes the Milagro *reposado* and the Centinela *añejo*. Some other high-end brands worth seeking out: Gran Centenario, Chinaco, Don Julio, Herradura, and Tres Generaciones. All of these tequilas are worthy of a snifter as opposed to a shot glass.

Patrón was not the first premium tequila (Don Julio is more than 60 years old, and Robert Denton created Chinaco in 1983), but it virtually created the market in this country— where tequila was long regarded as gnarly frat-house buzz fuel—thanks in no small measure to DeJoria's marketing genius and his Hollywood connections. His friend Wolfgang Puck held a tequila tasting at Spago's in 1991, which Patrón won handily, while his friend Clint Eastwood showed the bottle in his 1993 film *In the Line of Fire*. I remember Patrón as the insider's secret at the Beverly Hills nightclub Tattoo in the early '90s. Of the 21 million liters of 100 percent agave tequila produced last year, more than 7 million were Patrón. Premium tequila represents just 5 percent of the total production, but it is by far the fastest-growing part of the market in the United States. Clearly, it's not just for spring break anymore.

PREMIUM TEQUILAS

1 HERRADURA AÑEJO
Like a peaty single malt. Very smoky and complex, but no one would call it smooth. If it were a wine, it would be a Châteauneuf-du-Pape. $50.

2 PATRÓN CITRÓNGE
The ideal orange liqueur for an outstanding margarita: one part Citronge, one part Patrón silver, and fresh lime to taste. $30.

3 PATRÓN SILVER TEQUILA
Smooth and sippable, with a nice core of agave flavor. The perfect base for a margarita. $58.

4 GRAN CENTENARIO AÑEJO Smoky, woody, and nutty—if you're a blended-scotch drinker, you'll love it. $55.

5 CHINACO BLANCO
Great, almost aggressive agave flavor. Drink it neat. $52.

6 DON JULIO 1942 TEQUILA AÑEJO Layers of butterscotch and vanilla on top of the agave. Rich and smooth. Cries out for a brandy snifter. $130.

Charles Dickens's first visit to the New World

By Gloria Deák

He was the darling of the media on both sides of the Atlantic, and who can wonder? While still in his twenties, Charles Dickens had conceived five novels teeming with new ideas and bulging with characters as colorful as they were original. Who had not heard of the irrepressible Samuel Pickwick, wandering chairman of the Pickwick Club; or of the gentle Oliver Twist, orphaned and frightened, who dared to ask for more? Or of suave Mr. Mantalini and strolling Miss Snevellicci in the wide Nicholas Nickleby circle? Who had not shed tears as they followed the serialized fate of Little Nell, begging her creator by mail not to let her die in the final segment? Such storied characters were as familiar to the minds and hearts of a multitude of readers as was the name of the author himself. And now, in January 1842, the twenty-nine-year-old Dickens was ready to board a steam packet, brave the winter terrors of the